THE BUL

]

By WILL

UNITED STATES SENATE, COMMITTEE ON FOREIGN RELATIONS,

Washington, D.C., Friday, September 12, 1919.

The committee met, pursuant to the call of the chairman, at 10 o'clock a.m., in room 310, Senate Office Building, Senator Henry Cabot Lodge presiding.

Present: Senators Lodge (chairman), Brandegee, Fall, Knox, Harding, and New.

The CHAIRMAN. Mr. Bullitt is to make a statement to the committee this morning. I think I ought to say that Mr. Bullitt was summoned on the 23d of August, I believe, and he was in the woods at that time, out of reach of telegraph or telephone or mail, and only received the summons a few days ago. He came at once to Washington. That is the reason of the delay in his hearing.

The CHAIRMAN. Mr. Bullitt, will you take the stand and give your full name, please, to the stenographer?

Mr. BULLITT, William C. Bullitt.

The CHAIRMAN. You are a native and a resident of Philadelphia, are you not?

Mr. BULLITT. I am, sir.

The CHAIRMAN. Prior to the war, what were you engaged in?

Mr. BULLITT. Before the war I was employed by the Philadelphia Public Ledger. I had been a correspondent for them in various places, and I had been a member of the editorial staff in Philadelphia for a time.

The CHAIRMAN. You went abroad for them as a correspondent?

Mr. BULLITT. I did, sir.

The CHAIRMAN. Before we went into the war?

Mr. BULLITT. Before we went into the war I toured Germany, Austria, Hungary, Belgium, Poland, and other places, studying conditions there, for the purposes of the Public Ledger.

The CHAIRMAN. After we entered the war, what did you do? You came back?

Mr. BULLITT. Yes, sir; I came back. I was in the United States at that time.

The CHAIRMAN. At that time?

Mr. BULLITT. And I was asked to enter the Department of State, to work in the Division of Western European Affairs under Mr. Grew, in which my special province was to follow the political situation of Germany and Austria-Hungary, to prepare the confidential reports of the department on Germany, Austria, and Hungary—the weekly reports—and also such memoranda on conditions as the President and the Secretary and others might call for.

The CHAIRMAN. And then you went to Paris as a member of the staff, after the armistice?

Mr. BULLITT. Yes; I was an employee of the department at the time of the armistice, and I was ordered to Paris as a member of the staff of the commission.

Senator KNOX. When did you first go to Paris, Mr. Bullitt?

Mr. BULLITT. I sailed on the *George Washington*. I went over with the original trip of the President.

Senator KNOX. And you were there continuously how long?

Mr. BULLITT. I remained in Paris until—I can give you the exact date—I was ordered to go on a special mission to Berne about the first week of February. I can give you the exact date, if it is of any moment.

Senator KNOX. No; it is not.

Mr. BULLITT. I remained a week in Berne, then returned and remained in Paris until I was ordered to go to Russia.

I left for Russia on the 22d of February. I was in Paris during the entire period until the 22d of February. Senator KNOX. You said you went over on the original trip of the President. Just to get these dates right, when did you reach Paris?

Mr. BULLITT. I left New York on December 4 and, as I remember, we reached Paris on December 13.

Senator KNOX. And you were there, then, until you went to Berne in February?

Mr. BULLITT. In February.

Senator KNOX. What was your personal relation to the peace conference and its work?

MR. BULLITT'S OFFICIAL STATUS

Mr. BULLITT. When I first arrived I was asked to take charge of a confidential bulletin which was to be gotten out for the benefit of the commissioners each morning. It was to be read by them. That lasted a very short time, and as is usual with most things of the kind, we discovered that the commissioners did not care to spend the time reading it, and therefore it was decided to abolish this bulletin, and that instead I should receive all the intelligence reports of military intelligence, of the State Department, intelligence received through all the special dispatches of the ambassadors, etc., in fact, all the information that came in, and a section was created called the Current Intelligence Section. I was called the Chief of the Division of Current Intelligence Summaries.

Senator KNOX. Then, as I understand, your function was to acquaint yourself with everything that was going on in connection with the conference, and disseminate the news to the different branches of the peace conference and the different bureaus?

Mr. BULLITT. I was to report only to the commissioners.

Senator KNOX. Well, but the essential thing is, was it your duty to get information?

Mr. BULLITT. Yes; it was my duty to be in constant touch with everyone who was in the American delegation, and present information to the commissioners each morning. I had 20 minutes with each commissioner each morning.

Senator KNOX. So that you were practically a clearing house of information for the members of the American mission?

Mr. BULLITT. That is what I was supposed to be.

* * * * *

ORDERED TO RUSSIA

Senator KNOX. What was your mission to Russia, and when did you go?

Mr. BULLITT. I was ordered to go to Russia on the 18th of February. I received the following order from Secretary Lansing [reading]:

AMERICAN COMMISSION TO NEGOTIATE PEACE,
18 February, 1919.
    MR. WILLIAM C. BULLITT,
American Commission to Negotiate Peace.

SIR: You are hereby directed to proceed to Russia for the purpose of studying conditions, political and economic, therein, for the benefit of the American commissioners plenipotentiary to negotiate peace, and all American diplomatic and consular officials are hereby directed to extend to you the proper courtesies and facilities to enable you to fulfill the duties of your mission.

I am, sir, your obedient servant,
    ROBERT LANSING,
Secretary of State of the United States of America.
[SEAL.]

Senator KNOX. What is the date of that?

Mr. BULLITT. February 18, 1919. I also received at the same time from Mr. Joseph C. Grew, the secretary of the American commission, the following [reading]:

AMERICAN COMMISSION TO NEGOTIATE PEACE,
18 February, 1919.

To whom it may concern:

I hereby certify that Mr. William C. Bullitt has been authorized by the American commissioners plenipotentiary to negotiate peace to proceed to Russia, for the purpose of studying conditions, political and economic, therein, for the benefit of the commission, and I bespeak for him the proper courtesies and facilities in enabling him to fulfill the duties of his mission.

    J.C. GREW,
Secretary of the American Commission to Negotiate Peace.
[SEAL.]

Senator KNOX. You say you started in February. What time in February?

Mr. BULLITT. I left on the 22d day of February.

Senator KNOX. Did you know at that time, or have you ascertained since, whether a secret mission had or not been dispatched from Paris, that is, by the President himself; a man by the name of Buckler, who went to Russia a few days before you did?

Mr. BULLITT. Mr. W.H. Buckler, Mr. Henry White's half brother. He was an attaché of the American embassy in London. He was ordered from there to go, about the 1st of January, to Stockholm, to confer with Litvinov, who had been the Ambassador of the Soviet Government to

2

London—the British had allowed him to stay there without actually recognizing his official status, and had dealt with him

Mr. Buckler there conferred with Litvinov, who made various propositions and representations to him which Mr. Buckler at once telegraphed back to Paris, and which were considered so important by the President that the President read them in extenso to the council of ten on the morning of January 21. I regret that I have no actual copy of those proposals by Litvinov, or of Buckler's telegrams. At that time there was a discussion taking place in regard to Russia which had extended over a couple of weeks, a discussion of the utmost interest, in the council of ten. I happen to have the minutes of the council for January 16, when this Russian question was taken up, which I shall be glad to read, if the Senators should be interested, and also the minutes of the council of ten on January 21, at which meeting the Prinkipos proposal was decided upon. The Buckler meeting with Litvinov was what eventually swung the meeting in favor of Prinkipos, the suggestion for which had been made by Mr. Lloyd George. No; that is slightly incorrect. Mr. Lloyd George had suggested that representatives of the various Russian governments and factions should be brought to Paris.

COUNCIL OF TEN DISCUSSES RUSSIA

NOTES ON CONVERSATIONS HELD IN THE OFFICE OF M. PICHON AT THE QUAI D'ORSAY, ON JANUARY 16, 1919—PRELIMINARY DISCUSSION REGARDING THE SITUATION IN RUSSIA.

Mr. Lloyd George commenced his statement setting forth the information in the possession of the British Government regarding the Russian situation, by referring to the matter which had been exposed recently in L'Humanite. He stated that he wished to point out that there had been a serious misconception on the part of the French Government as to the character of the proposal of the British Government. The British proposal did not contemplate in any sense whatever, a recognition of the Bolsheviki Government, nor a suggestion that Bolshevik delegates be invited to attend the Conference. The British proposal was to invite all of the different governments now at war within what used to be the Russian Empire, to a truce of God, to stop reprisals and outrages and to send men here to give, so to speak, an account of themselves. The Great Powers would then try to find a way to bring some order out of chaos. These men were not to be delegates to the Peace Conference, and he agreed with the French Government entirely that they should not be made members of the Conference.

Mr. Lloyd George then proceeded to set forth briefly the reasons which had led the British Government to make this proposal. They were as follows:

Firstly, the real facts are not known;

Secondly, it is impossible to get the facts, the only way is to adjudicate the question; and

Thirdly, conditions in Russia are very bad; there is general mis-government and starvation. It is not known who is obtaining the upper hand, but the hope that the Bolshevik Government would collapse had not been realized. In fact, there is one report that the Bolsheviki are stronger than ever, that their internal position is strong, and that their hold on the people is stronger. Take, for instance, the case of the Ukraine. Some adventurer raises a few men and overthrows the Government. The Government is incapable of overthrowing him. It is also reported that the peasants are becoming Bolsheviki. It is hardly the business of the Great Powers to intervene either in lending financial support to one side or the other, or in sending munitions to either side.

Mr. Lloyd George stated that there seemed to be three possible policies:

1. Military intervention. It is true there the Bolsheviki movement is as dangerous to civilization as German militarism, but as to putting it down by the sword, is there anyone who proposes it? It would mean holding a certain number of vast provinces in Russia. The Germans with one million men on their Eastern Front only held the fringe of this territory. If he now proposed to send a thousand British troops to Russia for that purpose, the armies would mutiny. The same applies to U.S. troops in Siberia; also to Canadians and French as well. The mere idea of crushing Bolshevism by a military force is pure madness. Even admitting that it is done, who is to occupy Russia? No one can conceive or understand to bring about order by force.

2. A cordon. The second suggestion is to besiege Bolshevik Russia. Mr. Lloyd George wondered if those present realized what this would mean. From the information furnished him Bolshevik Russia has no corn, but within this territory there are 150,000,000 men, women, and

children. There is now starvation in Petrograd and Moscow. This is not a health cordon, it is a death cordon. Moreover, as a matter of fact, the people who would die are just the people that the Allies desire to protect. It would not result in the starvation of the Bolsheviki; it would simply mean the death of our friends. The cordon policy is a policy which, as humane people, those present could not consider.

Mr. Lloyd George asked who was there to overthrow the Bolsheviki? He had been told there were three men, Denekin, Kolchak and Knox. In considering the chances of these people to overthrow the Bolsheviki, he pointed out that he had received information that the Czecho-Slovaks now refused to fight; that the Russian Army was not to be trusted, and that while it was true that a Bolshevik Army had recently gone over to Kolchak it was never certain that just the reverse of this would not take place. If the Allies counted on any of these men, he believed they were building on quick-sand. He had heard a lot of talk about Denekin, but when he looked on the map he found that Denekin was occupying a little backyard near the Black Sea. Then he had been told that Denekin had recognized Kolchak, but when he looked on the map, there was a great solid block of territory between Denekin and Kolchak. Moreover, from information received it would appear that Kolchak had been collecting members of the old régime around him, and would seem to be at heart a monarchist. It appeared that the Czecho-Slovaks were finding this out. The sympathies of the Czecho-Slovaks are very democratic, and they are not at all prepared to fight for the restoration of the old conditions in Russia.

Mr. Lloyd George stated that he was informed that at the present time two-thirds of Bolshevik Russia was starving.

Institutions of Bolsheviki are institutions of old Czarist régime. This is not what one would call creating a new world.

3. The third alternative was contained in the British proposal, which was to summon these people to Paris to appear before those present, somewhat in the way that the Roman Empire summoned chiefs of outlying tributary states to render an account of their actions.

Mr. Lloyd George pointed out the fact that the argument might be used that there were already here certain representatives of these Governments; but take, for instance, the case of Sazonov, who claims to represent the Government of Omsk. As a matter of fact, Sazonov can not speak from personal observation. He is nothing but a partisan, like all the rest. He has never been in contact, and is not now in direct contact with the Government at Omsk.

It would be manifestly absurd for those who are responsible for bringing about the Peace Conference, to come to any agreement and leave Paris when one-half of Europe and one-half of Asia is still in flames. Those present must settle this question or make fools of themselves.

Mr. Lloyd George referred to the objection that had been raised to permitting Bolshevik delegates to come to Paris. It had been claimed that they would convert France and England to Bolshevism. If England becomes Bolshevist, it will not be because a single Bolshevist representative is permitted to enter England. On the other hand, if a military enterprise were started against the Bolsheviki, that would make England Bolshevist, and there would be a Soviet in London. For his part, Mr. Lloyd George was not afraid of Bolshevism if the facts are known in England and the United States. The same applied to Germany. He was convinced that an educated democracy can be always trusted to turn down Bolshevism.

Under all circumstances, Mr. Lloyd George saw no better way out than to follow the third alternative. Let the Great Powers impose their conditions and summon these people to Paris to give an account of themselves to the Great Powers, not to the Peace Conference.

Mr. Pichon suggested that it might be well to ask M. Noulens, the French Ambassador to Russia, who had just returned to France, to appear before the meeting to-morrow morning, and give those present his views on the Russian situation.

President Wilson stated that he did not see how it was possible to controvert the statement of Mr. Lloyd George. He thought that there was a force behind this discussion which was no doubt in his mind, but which it might be desirable to bring out a little more definitely. He did not believe that there would be sympathy anywhere with the brutal aspect of Bolshevism, if it were not for the fact of the domination of large vested interests in the political and economic world. While it might be true that this evil was in process of discussion and slow reform, it must be admitted, that the general body of men have grown impatient at the failure to bring about the necessary reform. He stated that there were many men who represented large vested interests in the United States who saw the necessity for these reforms and desired something which should be worked out at the Peace Conference, namely, the establishment of some machinery to provide for the opportunity of the individuals greater than the world has ever known. Capital and labor in the United States are not friends. Still they are not enemies in the sense that they are thinking of resorting to physical force to settle their differences. But they are distrustful, each of the other. Society can not go on that plane. On the one hand, there is a minority possessing capital and brains; on the other, a majority consisting of the great bodies of workers who are essential to the minority, but do not trust the minority, and feel that the minority will never render them their rights. A way must be found to put trust and cooperation between these two.

President Wilson pointed out that the whole world was disturbed by this question before the Bolsheviki came into power. Seeds need soil, and the Bolsheviki seeds found the soil already prepared for them.

President Wilson stated that he would not be surprised to find that the reason why British and United States troops would not be ready to enter Russia to fight the Bolsheviki was explained by the fact that the troops were not at all sure that if they put down Bolshevism they would not bring about a re-establishment of the ancient order. For example, in making a speech recently, to a well-dressed audience in New York City who were not to be expected to show such feeling, Mr. Wilson had referred casually to Russia, stating that the United States would do its utmost to aid her suppressed people. The audience exhibited the greatest enthusiasm, and this had remained in the President's mind as an index to where the sympathies of the New World are.

President Wilson believed that those present would be playing against the principle of the free spirit of the world if they did not give Russia a chance to find herself along the lines of utter freedom. He concurred with Mr. Lloyd George's view and supported his recommendations that the third line of procedure be adopted.

President Wilson stated that he had also, like Mr. Lloyd George, received a memorandum from his experts which agreed substantially with the information which Mr. Lloyd George had received. There was one point which he thought particularly worthy of notice, and that was the report that the strength of the Bolshevik leaders lay in the argument that if they were not supported by the people of Russia, there would be foreign intervention, and the Bolsheviki were the only thing that stood between the Russians and foreign military control. It might well be that if the Bolsheviki were assured that they were safe from foreign aggression, they might lose support of their own movement.

President Wilson further stated that he understood that the danger of destruction of all hope in the Baltic provinces was immediate, and that it should be made very clear if the British proposal were adopted, that the Bolsheviki would have to withdraw entirely from Lithuania and Poland. If they would agree to this to refrain from reprisals and outrages, he, for his part, would be prepared to receive representatives from as many groups and centers of action, as chose to come, and endeavor to assist them to reach a solution of their problem.

He thought that the British proposal contained the only suggestions that lead anywhere. It might lead nowhere. But this could at least be found out.

M. Pichon referred again to the suggestion that Ambassador Noulens be called before the meeting.

Mr. Balfour suggested that it might be well to call the Dutch Consul, lately in Petrograd, if it was the desire of those present to hear the anti-Bolshevik side.

Baron Sonnino suggested that M. Scavenius, Minister of Denmark, recently in Russia, would be able to give interesting data on the Russian situation.

Those present seemed to think that it might be desirable to hear what these gentlemen might have to say.

Senator KNOX. Do you know anything about a letter that Buckler wrote to the President in relation to his mission? Have you ever seen a copy of his report in the form of a letter?

Mr. BULLITT. I have read a copy of his report, but I have not the copy. The only reference I have to it that I find, in the short time I have had to go over my papers since I came down from the woods, is in a memorandum to Col. House in reference to the withdrawal of the American troops from Archangel [reading]:

Buckler discussed the matter of the withdrawal of these troops with Litvinov, who said that unquestionably the Bolsheviki would agree to an armistice on the Archangel front at any time; and, furthermore, would pledge themselves not to injure in any way those Russians in and about Archangel who have been cooperating with the Allies. He, furthermore, suggested that such Russians as did not care to trust their lives to such a promise should be taken out with the troops.

Senator KNOX. Do you know anything about whether Litvinov communicated directly with the President in reference to this Buckler mission?

Mr. BULLITT. Litvinov had written a letter to the President, which has since been widely published, on December 24.

Senator KNOX. That is the letter I had in mind. I had seen some references to that. Do you have a copy of that letter?

Mr. BULLITT. I do not know whether I have any copies of this letter—that is, authentic. I think I have a newspaper copy some place, but I have no actual copy of the letter.

Senator KNOX. Can you tell us anything more about the discussion in reference to the withdrawal of troops from Russia that took place at that time—anything more than is indicated by your letter, there?

Mr. BULLITT. There were very serious discussions, all the time. Telegrams were being received frequently from the various commanders at Archangel, the American and the British notably, in regard to conditions, which they described as likely to be disastrous, and discussions of real gravity were taking place all the time. The subject was very much in the air. I have, I will say, very few references to that particular condition. I have here this memorandum which takes up some of these subjects. I do not know if the committee would care to hear it.

The CHAIRMAN. Yes.

Senator KNOX. This is a memorandum that you sent to Col. House?

Mr. BULLITT. Yes; Col. House.

Senator KNOX. Please read it.

Mr. BULLITT [reading]:

JANUARY 30, 1919.

Memorandum for Col. House.

Subject: Withdrawal of American troops from Archangel.

DEAR COL. HOUSE: The 12,000 American, British, and French troops at Archangel are no longer serving any useful purpose. Only 3,000 Russians have rallied around this force. It is the attacked, not the attacker, and serves merely to create cynicism in regard to all our proposals and to stimulate recruiting for the Red Army.

Furthermore, the 4,000 Americans, 6,000 British, 2,000 French, and 3,000 Russian troops in this region are in considerable danger of destruction by the Bolsheviki. Gen. Ironside has just appealed for reinforcements and the British war office has directed the commanding general at Murmansk to be prepared to dispatch a battalion of Infantry to Archangel.

Instead of transferring troops from Murmansk to Archangel, it seems to me that we should at once transfer to Murmansk and bring home the troops which are now at Archangel. Aside from the needless suffering which these men are enduring, aside from the demands of the public in the United States and England for the return of these men, it seems to me that the withdrawal of these troops would be of great value as a proof that we have made the Prinkipos proposal in full good faith.

I have asked Gen. Churchill to obtain the most expert opinion available on the practicability of moving the 12,000 American, British, and French troops and such Russians as may wish to accompany them from Archangel to Murmansk. The appended memorandum and map which he has prepared show that unless the ice in the White Sea suddenly becomes thicker it is at present possible with the aid of six ice breakers which are now at Archangel to move these troops by water to Kem on the Murmansk Railroad, whence they may be carried by train to Murmansk.

Buckler discussed the matter of the withdrawal of these troops with Litvinov, who said that unquestionably the Bolsheviki would agree to an armistice on the Archangel front at any time and, furthermore, would pledge themselves not to injure in any way those Russians in and about Archangel who have been cooperating with the Allies. He furthermore suggested that such Russians as did not care to trust their lives to such a promise should be taken out with the troops.

6

The provisional government at Archangel has just notified us that it will not accept the proposal for a conference at Prinkipos. It seems dignified and honorable at this moment to inform the Archangel government that since it can not agree to the allied proposal, presented after the most serious consideration, we shall decline to support it further with arms, but will make provision for the safety of all Russians who are unwilling to remain at Archangel.

I have discussed this Archangel business at some length with Philip Kerr, Lloyd George's secretary, who says that L.G. intends to bring the British troops out on the 1st of May, which he believes to be the first practicable moment. The first practicable moment, however, seems to be now.

The situation at Archangel is most serious for the soldiers who are stationed there, but it is also serious for the Governments which sent them out and seem to have abandoned them. Unless they are saved by prompt action, we shall have another Gallipoli. Very respectfully yours,

WILLIAM C. BULLITT.

I discussed these matters with each one of the commissioners each morning. It was my duty to keep them au courant with anything that struck me as important, which in the stress of the business of the peace conference they were likely to overlook.

Senator KNOX. This was a memorandum made in the line of your duty?

Mr. BULLITT. This was a memorandum made as the result of the conversations that I had had with all of the commissioners that morning.

This particular memorandum, in fact, was ordered by Col. House, and in connection with it he asked me to have made a map showing the feasibility of getting the troops out of Russia, by the military experts of the conference, which map I have here. If you would be interested in it in any way, I will append the memorandum made for Gen. Churchill with regard to withdrawing the troops.

Senator KNOX. I was going to ask you whether or not you had any information as to the terms which the Allies were willing to accept from Russia.

COUNCIL OF TEN FORMULATES A RUSSIAN POLICY

Mr. BULLITT. I had, of course, seen the discussions of the conference with regard to the entire Russian matter. The conference had decided, after long consideration, that it was impossible to subdue or wipe out the Soviet Government by force. The discussion of that is of a certain interest, I believe, in connection with this general matter. There are, in regard to the question you have just asked, minutes of the council of ten, on January 21, 1919.

Lloyd George had introduced the proposition that representatives of the Soviet Government should be brought to Paris along with the representatives of the other Russian governments [reading]:

[McD. Secret. I.C. 114. Secretaries' notes of a conversation held in M. Pichon's room at the Quai d'Orsay on Tuesday, January 21, 1919, at 15 hours.]

PRESENT

United States of America: President Wilson, Mr. R. Lansing, Mr. A.H. Frazier, Col. U.S. Grant, Mr. L. Harrison.

British Empire: The Right Hon. D. Lloyd George, The Right Hon. A.J. Balfour, Lieut. Col. Sir M.P.A. Hankey, K.C.B., Maj. A.M. Caccia, M.V.O., Mr. E. Phipps.

France: M. Clemenceau, M. Pichon, M. Dutasta, M. Berthelot, Capt. A. Potier.

Italy: Signor Orlando, H.E. Baron Sonnino, Count Aldrovandi, Maj. A. Jones.

Japan: Baron Makino, H.E.M. Matsui, M. Saburi.

Interpreter, Prof. P.J. Mantoux.

SITUATION IN RUSSIA

M. Clemenceau said they had met together to decide what could be done in Russia under present circumstances.

President Wilson said that in order to have something definite to discuss, he wished to take advantage of a suggestion made by Mr. Lloyd George and to propose a modification of the British proposal. He wished to suggest that the various organized groups in Russia should be asked to send representatives, not to Paris, but to some other place, such as Salonika, convenient of approach, there to meet such representatives as might be appointed by the Allies, in order to see if they could draw up a program upon which agreement could be reached.

Mr. Lloyd George pointed out that the advantage of this would be that they could be brought straight there from Russia through the Black Sea without passing through other countries.

M. Sonnino said that some of the representatives of the various Governments were already here in Paris, for example, M. Sazonov. Why should these not be heard?

President Wilson expressed the view that the various parties should not be heard separately. It would be very desirable to get all these representatives in one place, and still better, all in one room, in order to obtain a close comparison of views.

Mr. Balfour said that a further objection to Mr. Sonnino's plan was that if M. Sazonov was heard in Paris, it would be difficult to refuse to hear the others in Paris also, and M. Clemenceau objected strongly to having some of these representatives in Paris.

M. Sonnino explained that all the Russian parties had some representatives here, except the Soviets, whom they did not wish to hear.

Mr. Lloyd George remarked that the Bolshevists were the very people some of them wished to hear.

M. Sonnino continuing said that they had heard M. Litovnov's statements that morning.

That was the statement that Litvinov had made to Buckler which the President had read to the council of ten that morning.

[Continuing reading.]

The Allies were now fighting against the Bolshevists who were their enemies, and therefore they were not obliged to hear them with the others.

Mr. Balfour remarked that the essence of President Wilson's proposal was that the parties must all be heard at one and the same time.

Mr. Lloyd George expressed the view that the acceptance of M. Sonnino's proposals would amount to their hearing a string of people, all of whom held the same opinion, and all of whom would strike the same note. But they would not hear the people who at the present moment were actually controlling European Russia. In deference to M. Clemenceau's views, they had put forward this new proposal. He thought it would be quite safe to bring the Bolshevist representatives to Salonika, or perhaps to Lemnos.

It was absolutely necessary to endeavor to make peace. The report read by President Wilson that morning went to show that the Bolshevists were not convinced of the error of their ways, but they apparently realised the folly of their present methods. Therefore they were endeavouring to come to terms.

President Wilson asked to be permitted to urge one aspect of the case. As M. Sonnino had implied, they were all repelled by Bolshevism, and for that reason they had placed armed men in opposition to them. One of the things that was clear in the Russian situation was that by opposing Bolshevism with arms, they were in reality serving the cause of Bolshevism. The Allies were making it possible for the Bolsheviks to argue that Imperialistic and Capitalistic Governments were endeavouring to exploit the country and to give the land back to the landlords, and so bring about a re-action. If it could be shown that this was not true, and that the Allies were prepared to deal with the rulers of Russia, much of the moral force of this argument would disappear. The allegation that the Allies were against the people and wanted to control their affairs provided the argument which enabled them to raise armies. If, on the other hand, the Allies could swallow their pride and the natural repulsion which they felt for the Bolshevists and see the representatives of all organized groups in one place, he thought it would bring about a marked reaction against Bolshevism.

M. Clemenceau said that, in principle, he did not favour conversation with the Bolshevists; not because they were criminals, but because we would be raising them to our level by saying that they were worthy of entering into conversation with us. The Bolshevist danger was very great at the present moment. Bolshevism was spreading. It had invaded the Baltic Provinces and Poland, and that very morning they received very bad news regarding its spread to Budapesth and Vienna. Italy, also, was in danger. The danger was probably greater there than in France. If Bolshevism, after spreading in Germany, were to traverse Austria and Hungary and so reach Italy, Europe would be faced with a very great danger. Therefore, something must be done against Bolshevism. When listening to the document presented by President Wilson that morning, he had been struck by the cleverness with which the Bolshevists were attempting to lay a trap for the Allies. When the Bolshevists first came into power, a breach was made with the Capitalist Government on questions of principle, but now they offered funds and concessions as a basis for treating with them. He need not say how valueless their promises were, but if they were listened to, the Bolshevists would go back to their people and say: "We offered them great principles of justice and the Allies would have nothing to do with us. Now we offer money, and they are ready to make peace."

He admitted his remarks did not offer a solution. The great misfortune was that the Allies were in need of a speedy solution. After four years of war, and the losses and sufferings they had incurred, their populations could stand no more. Russia also was in need of immediate peace. But its necessary evolution must take time. The signing of the world Peace could not await Russia's final avatar. Had time been available, he would suggest waiting, for eventually sound men representing common-sense would come to the top. But when would that be? He could make no forecast. Therefore they must press for an early solution.

To sum up, had he been acting by himself, he would temporize and erect barriers to prevent Bolshevism from spreading. But he was not alone, and in the presence of his colleagues he felt compelled to make some concession, as it was essential that there should not be even the appearance of disagreement amongst them. The concession came easier after having heard President Wilson's suggestions. He thought that they should make a very clear and convincing appeal to all reasonable peoples, emphatically stating that they did not wish in any way to interfere in the internal affairs of Russia, and especially that they had no intention of restoring Czardom. The object of the Allies being to hasten the creation of a strong Government, they proposed to call together representatives of all parties to a Conference. He would beg President Wilson to draft a paper, fully explaining the position of the Allies to the whole world, including the Russians and the Germans.

Mr. Lloyd George agreed and gave notice that he wished to withdraw his own motion in favour of President Wilson's.

Mr. Balfour said that he understood that all these people were to be asked on an equality. On these terms he thought the Bolshevists would refuse, and by their refusal, they would put themselves in a very bad position.

M. Sonnino said that he did not agree that the Bolshevists would not come. He thought they would be the first to come, because they would be eager to put themselves on an equality with the others. He would remind his colleagues that, before the Peace of Brest-Litovsk was signed, the Bolshevists promised all sorts of things, such as to refrain from propaganda, but since that peace had been concluded they had broken all their promises, their one idea being to spread revolution in all other countries. His idea was to collect together all the anti-Bolshevik parties and help them to make a strong Government, provided they pledged themselves not to serve the forces of re-action and especially not to touch the land question, thereby depriving the Bolshevists of their strongest argument. Should they take these pledges, he would be prepared to help them.

Mr. Lloyd George enquired how this help would be given.

M. Sonnino replied that help would be given with soldiers to a reasonable degree or by supplying arms, food, and money. For instance, Poland asked for weapons and munitions; the Ukraine asked for weapons. All the Allies wanted was to establish a strong Government. The reason that no strong Government at present existed was that no party could risk taking the offensive against Bolshevism without the assistance of the Allies. He would enquire how the parties of order could possibly succeed without the help of the Allies. President Wilson had said that they should put aside all pride in the matter. He would point out that, for Italy and probably for France also, as M. Clemenceau had stated, it was in reality a question of self-defence. He thought that even a partial recognition of the Bolshevists would strengthen their position, and, speaking for himself, he thought that Bolshevism was already a serious danger in his country.

Mr. Lloyd George said he wished to put one or two practical questions to M. Sonnino. The British Empire now had some 15,000 to 20,000 men in Russia. M. de Scavenius had estimated that some 150,000 additional men would be required, in order to keep the anti-Bolshevist Governments from dissolution. And General Franchet d'Esperey also insisted on the necessity of Allied assistance. Now Canada had decided to withdraw her troops, because the Canadian soldiers would not agree to stay and fight against the Russians. Similar trouble had also occurred amongst the other Allied troops. And he felt certain that, if the British tried to send any more troops there, there would be mutiny.

M. Sonnino suggested that volunteers might be called for.

Mr. Lloyd George, continuing, said that it would be impossible to raise 150,000 men in that way. He asked, however, what contributions America, Italy and France would make towards the raising of this Army.

President Wilson and M. Clemenceau each said none.

M. Orlando agreed that Italy could make no further contributions.

Mr. Lloyd George said that the Bolshevists had an army of 300,000 men who would, before long, be good soldiers, and to fight them at least 400,000 Russian soldiers would be required. Who would feed, equip and pay them? Would Italy, or America, or France, do so? If they were unable to do that, what would be the good of fighting Bolshevism? It could not be crushed by speeches. He sincerely trusted that they would accept President Wilson's proposal as it now stood.

M. Orlando agreed that the question was a very difficult one for the reasons that had been fully given. He agreed that Bolshevism constituted a grave danger to all Europe. To prevent a contagious epidemic from spreading, the sanitarians set up a *cordon Sanitaire*. If similar measures could be taken against Bolshevism, in order to prevent its spreading, it might be overcome, since to isolate it meant vanquishing it. Italy was now passing through a period of depression, due to war weariness. But Bolshevists could never triumph there, unless they found a favourable medium, such as might be produced either by a profound patriotic disappointment in their expectations as to the rewards of the war, or by an economic crisis. Either might lead to revolution, which was equivalent to Bolshevism. Therefore, he would insist that all possible measures should be taken to set up this cordon. Next, he suggested the consideration of repressive measures. He thought two methods were possible; either the use of physical force or the use of moral force. He thought Mr. Lloyd George's objection to the use of physical force unanswerable. The occupation of Russia meant the employment of large numbers of troops for an indefinite period of time. This meant an apparent prolongation of the war. There remained the use of moral force. He agreed with M. Clemenceau that no country could continue in anarchy and that an end must eventually come; but they could not wait; they could not proceed to make peace and ignore Russia. Therefore, Mr. Lloyd George's proposal, with the modifications introduced after careful consideration by President Wilson and M. Clemenceau, gave a possible solution. It did not involve entering into negotiations with the Bolsheviks; the proposal was merely an attempt to bring together all the parties in Russia with a view to finding a way out of the present difficulty. He was prepared, therefore, to support it.

President Wilson asked for the views of his Japanese colleagues.

Baron Makino said that after carefully considering the various points of view put forward, he had no objections to make regarding the conclusions reached. He thought that was the best solution under the circumstances. He wished, however, to enquire what attitude would be taken by the Representatives of the Allied powers if the Bolshevists accepted the invitation to the meeting and there insisted upon their principles. He thought they should under no circumstances countenance Bolshevist ideas. The conditions in Siberia East of the Baikal had greatly improved. The objects which had necessitated the despatch of troops to that region had been attained. Bolshevism was no longer aggressive, though it might still persist in a latent form. In conclusion, he wished to support the proposal before the meeting.

President Wilson expressed the view that the emissaries of the Allied Powers should not be authorised to adopt any definite attitude towards Bolshevism. They should merely report back to their Governments the conditions found.

Mr. Lloyd George asked that that question be further considered. He thought the emissaries of the Allied Powers should be able to establish an agreement if they were able to find a solution. For instance, if they succeeded in reaching an agreement on the subject of the organization of a Constituent Assembly, they should be authorised to accept such a compromise without the delay of a reference to the Governments.

President Wilson suggested that the emissaries might be furnished with a body of instructions.

Mr. Balfour expressed the view that abstention from hostile action against their neighbours should be made a condition of their sending representatives to this meeting.

President Wilson agreed.

M. Clemenceau suggested that the manifesto to the Russian parties should be based solely on humanitarian grounds. They should say to the Russians: "You are threatened by famine. We are prompted by humanitarian feelings; we are making peace; we do not want people to die. We are prepared to see what can be done to remove the menace of starvation." He thought the Russians would at once prick up their ears, and be prepared to hear what the Allies had to say. They would add that food cannot be sent unless peace and order were re-established. It should, in fact, be made quite clear that the representatives of all parties would merely be brought together for purely humane reasons.

Mr. Lloyd George said that in this connection he wished to invite attention to a doubt expressed by certain of the delegates of the British Dominions, namely, whether there would be enough food and credit to go round should an attempt be made to feed all Allied countries, and enemy countries, and Russia also. The export of so much food would inevitably have the effect of raising food prices in Allied countries and so create discontent and Bolshevism. As regards grain, Russia had always been an exporting country, and there was evidence to show that plenty of food at present existed in the Ukraine.

President Wilson said that his information was that enough food existed in Russia, but, either on account of its being hoarded or on account of difficulties of transportation, it could not be made available.

(It was agreed that President Wilson should draft a proclamation, for consideration at the next meeting, inviting all organized parties in Russia to attend a Meeting to be held at some selected place such as Salonika or Lemnos, in order to discuss with the representatives of the Allied and Associated Great Powers the means of restoring order and peace in Russia. Participation in the Meeting should be conditional on a cessation of hostilities.)

2. *Peace Conference.*—M. Clemenceau considered it to be most urgent that the delegates should be set to work. He understood that President Wilson would be ready to put on the table at the next full Conference, proposals relating to the creation of a League of Nations. He was anxious to add a second question, which could be studied immediately, namely, reparation for damages. He thought the meeting should consider how the work should be organized in order to give effect to this suggestion.

Mr. Lloyd George said that he agreed that these questions should be studied forthwith. He would suggest that, in the first place, the League of Nations should be considered, and, that after the framing of the principles, an International Committee of Experts be set to work out its constitution in detail. The same remark applied also to the question of indemnities and reparation. He thought that a Committee should also be appointed as soon as possible to consider International Labour Legislation.

President Wilson observed that he had himself drawn up a constitution of a League of Nations. He could not claim that it was wholly his own creation. Its generation was as follows:—He had received the Phillimore Report, which had been amended by Colonel House and re-written by himself. He had again revised it after having received General Smuts' and Lord Robert Cecil's reports. It was therefore a compound of these various suggestions. During the week he had seen M. Bourgeois, with whom he found himself to be in substantial accord on principles. A few days ago he had discussed his draft with Lord Robert Cecil and General Smuts, and they found themselves very near together.

Mr. Balfour suggested that President Wilson's draft should be submitted to the Committee as a basis for discussion.

President Wilson further suggested that the question should be referred as far as possible to the men who had been studying it.

Mr. Lloyd George expressed his complete agreement. He thought they themselves should, in the first place, agree on the fundamental principles and then refer the matter to the

11

Committee. When that Committee met they could take President Wilson's proposals as the basis of discussion.

(It was agreed that the question of appointing an International Committee, consisting of two members from each of the five Great Powers, to whom would be referred President Wilson's draft, with certain basic principles to guide them, should be considered at the next meeting.)

3. *Poland.*—M. Pichon called attention to the necessity for replying to the demand addressed by M. Paderewski to Colonel House, which had been read by President Wilson that morning, and asked that Marshal Foch should be present.

(It was agreed that this question should be discussed at the next Meeting.)

4. *Disarmament.*—Mr. Balfour called attention to the urgency of the question of disarmament, and said that he would shortly propose that a Committee should be appointed to consider this question.

VILLA MAJESTIC, Paris January 21st, 1919.

This is the minute of January 21, and the Prinkipos memorandum was written on January 22. The instructions to the President were as follows:

It was agreed that President Wilson should draft a proclamation for consideration at the next meeting, inviting all organized parties in Russia to attend a meeting to be held at some selected place such as Salonika or Lemnos, in order to discuss with the representatives of the allied and associated great powers the means of restoring order and peace in Russia. Participation in the meeting should be conditional on a cessation of hostilities.

The President then wrote the Prinkipos proposition.

Senator KNOX. Did you make a written report of your mission?

Mr. BULLITT. I did, sir.

Senator KNOX. Have you it here?

Mr. BULLITT. Yes, sir. I might read the report without the appendices.

Senator KNOX. The chairman wants you to read it.

The CHAIRMAN. I do not know whether it is very long. The report he made would be of some interest. You were the only official representative sent?

Mr. BULLITT. Yes, sir; except Capt. Pettit, my assistant. The circumstances of my sending will perhaps require further elucidation. I not only was acquainted with the minutes of the discussions of the council of ten, but in addition I had discussed the subject with each of the commissioners each morning and I had talked with many British representatives. After the Prinkipos proposal was made, the replies began to come in from various factions, that they would refuse to accept it for various reasons. The Soviet Government replied in a slightly evasive form. They said, "We are ready to accept the terms of the proposals, and we are ready to talk about stopping fighting." They did not say, "We are ready to stop fighting on such and such a date." It was not made specific.

Senator KNOX. That was one of the conditions of the proposal?

FRANCE BLOCKS PRINKIPOS CONFERENCE

Mr. BULLITT. It was. That is why I say they replied in an evasive manner. The French—and particularly the French foreign office, even more than Mr. Clemenceau—and you can observe it from that minute were opposed to the idea, and we found that the French foreign office had communicated to the Ukrainian Government and various other antisoviet governments that if they were to refuse the proposal, they would support them and continue to support them, and not allow the Allies, if they could prevent it, or the allied Governments, to make peace with the Russian Soviet Government.

At all events, the time set for the Prinkipos proposal was February 15. At that time nobody had acted in a definite, uncompromising matter. It therefore fell to the ground.

There was a further discussion as to what should be done. The peace conference was still of the opinion that it was impossible to hope to conquer the Soviet Government by force of arms, because in the latter part of that report, which I did not read to the committee, there was expressed very forcibly the opinion of Mr. Lloyd George, that the populations at home would not stand it. Therefore they desired to follow up further the line of making peace.

12

About that time I was working particularly closely on the Russian affairs. I had had a number of discussions with everyone concerned in it, and on the very day that Col. House and Mr. Lansing first asked me to undertake this mission to Russia, I was dining at Mr. Lloyd George's apartment to discuss Russian affairs with his secretaries, so that I had a fair idea of the point of view of everyone in Paris.

I further, before I went, received urgent instructions from Secretary Lansing if possible to obtain the release of Consul Treadwell, who had been our consul in Petrograd and had been transferred to Tashkent, and had been detained by the local Soviet Government and had been kept there several months. He was one of our Government officers they had seized. Mr. Lansing ordered me to do everything I could to obtain his release.

I further, before I went, asked Col. House certain specific questions in regard to what, exactly, the point of view of our Government was on this subject, what we were ready to do, and I think it perhaps might be important to detail a brief resume of this conversation. The idea was this: Lloyd George had gone over to London on February 9, as I remember, to try to adjust some labor troubles. He, however, still insisted that the Prinkipos proposal must be renewed or some other peace proposal must be made, and I arranged a meeting between him and Col. House, which was to take place, I believe, on February 24, at which time they were to prepare a renewal of the Prinkipos proposal, and they were both prepared to insist that it be passed against any opposition of the French.

I arranged this meeting through Mr. Philip Kerr, Mr. Lloyd George's confidential assistant. However, on the 19th day of the month, Mr. Clemenceau was shot, and the next day Mr. Lloyd George telephoned over from London to say that as long as Clemenceau was wounded and was ill, he was boss of the roost, and that anything he desired to veto would be immediately wiped out and therefore it was no use for him and Col. House, as long as Clemenceau was ill, to attempt to renew the Prinkipos proposal, as Clemenceau would simply have to hold up a finger and the whole thing would drop to the ground. Therefore, it was decided that I should go at once to Russia to attempt to obtain from the Soviet Government an exact statement of the terms on which they were ready to stop fighting. I was ordered if possible to obtain that statement and have it back in Paris before the President returned to Paris from the United States. The plan was to make a proposal to the Soviet Government which would certainly be accepted.

The CHAIRMAN. These orders came from the President?

Mr. BULLITT. These orders came to me from Col. House. I also discussed the matter with Mr. Lansing, and Mr. Lansing and Col. House gave me the instructions which I had.

Senator KNOX. You said a moment ago that you went to Col. House to get a statement of the American position.

WHAT AMERICA WANTED

Mr. BULLITT. Yes; I asked Col. House these questions [reading]:

1. If the Bolsheviki are ready to stop the forward movement of their troops on all fronts and to declare an armistice on all fronts, would we be willing to do likewise?

2. Is the American Government prepared to insist that the French, British, Italian, and Japanese Governments shall accept such an armistice proposal?

3. If fighting is stopped on all fronts, is the Government of the United States prepared to insist on the reestablishment of economic relations with Russia, subject only to the equitable distribution among all classes of the population of supplies and food and essential commodities which may be sent to Russia?

In other words, a sort of Hoover Belgian distribution plan so that the Bolsheviki could not use the food we sent in there for propaganda purposes and to starve their enemies and to feed their friends.

The fourth question I asked him was as follows:

4. Is the United States Government, under these conditions, prepared to press the Allies for a joint statement that all Allied troops will be withdrawn from the soil of Russia as soon as practicable, on condition that the Bolsheviki give explicit assurances that there will be no retaliation against persons who have cooperated with the allied forces?

Col. House replied that we were prepared to.

13

Further, I asked Col. House whether it was necessary to get a flat and explicit assurance from the Soviet Government that they would make full payment of all their debts before we would make peace with them, and Col. House replied that it was not; that no such statement was necessary, however, that such a statement would be extremely desirable to have, inasmuch as much of the French opposition to making peace with the Soviet Government was on account of the money owed by Russia to France.

I further had an intimation of the British disposition toward Russia. As I said before, I had discussed the matter with Mr. Philip Kerr, and Sir Maurice Hankey and Col. House asked me to inform Mr. Kerr of my mission before I went. It was to be an entire secret from all except the British. The British and American delegations worked in very close touch throughout the conference, and there were practically no secrets that the American delegation had that were not also the property of the British delegation.

THE BRITISH TERMS

I was asked to inform Mr. Kerr of this trip. I told him all about it, and asked him if he could get Mr. Balfour and Mr. Lloyd George to give me a general indication of their point of view on peace with Russia; what they would be prepared to do in the matter.

Mr. Kerr and I then talked and prepared what we thought might be the basis of peace with Russia.

I then received from Mr. Kerr, before I left, the following letter, which is a personal letter, which I regret greatly to bring forward, but which I feel is necessary in the interest of an understanding of this matter. [Reading:]

[Private and confidential.]

BRITISH DELEGATION,

Paris, February 21, 1919.

MY DEAR BULLITT: I inclose a note of the sort of conditions upon which I personally think it would be possible for the allied Governments to resume once more normal relations with Soviet Russia. You will understand, of course, that these have no official significance and merely represent suggestions of my own opinion.

Yours, sincerely,

P.H. KERR.

That was from Mr. Kerr, Lloyd George's confidential secretary. Mr. Kerr had, however, told me that he had discussed the entire matter with Mr. Lloyd George and Mr. Balfour, and therefore I thought he had a fair idea of what conditions the British were ready to accept. The note inclosed reads as follows:

1. Hostilities to cease on all fronts.

2. All de facto governments to remain in full control of the territories which they at present occupy.

3. Railways and ports necessary to transportation between soviet Russia and the sea to be subject to the same regulations as international railways and ports in the rest of Europe.

4. Allied subjects to be given free right of entry and full security to enable them to enter soviet Russia and go about their business there provided they do not interfere in politics.

5. Amnesty to all political prisoners on both sides: full liberty to all Russians who have fought with the Allies.

6. Trade relations to be restored between soviet Russia and the outside world under conditions which, while respecting the sovereignty of soviet Russia insure that allied supplies are made available on equal terms to all classes of the Russian people.

7. All other questions connected with Russia's debt to the Allies, etc., to be considered independently after peace has been established.

8. All allied troops to be withdrawn from Russia as soon as Russian armies above quota to be defined have been demobilized and their surplus arms surrendered or destroyed.

You will see the American and British positions were very close together.

Senator KNOX. With these statements from Col. House as to the American position and from Mr. Kerr as to the British position, and with the instructions which you had received, you proceeded to Russia, and, as you said a moment ago, you made a written report?

Mr. BULLITT. I did, sir. Do you want it read, or shall I state the substance and then put it in the record? I think I can state it more briefly if I read the first eight pages of it and then put the rest of it in the record.

The CHAIRMAN. Very well; do that.

Mr. BULLITT. This report I made to the President and to the American commissioners, by order of the President transmitted to me on my return by Mr. Lansing. I should like to say, before I read this report, that of course I was in Russia an extremely short time, and this is merely the best observation that I could make supplemented by the observation of Capt. Pettit of the Military Intelligence, who was sent in as my assistant, and with other impressions that I got from Mr. Lincoln Steffens and other observers who were there.

Senator KNOX. How long were you in Russia?

Mr. BULLITT. For only one week. I was instructed to go in and bring back as quickly as possible a definite statement of exactly the terms the Soviet Government was ready to accept. The idea in the minds of the British and the American delegation were that if the Allies made another proposal it should be a proposal which we would know in advance would be accepted, so that there would be no chance of another Prinkipos proposal miscarrying.

I might perhaps read first, or show to you, the official text. This is the official text of their proposition which they handed me in Moscow on the 14th of March. Here is a curious thing—the Soviet foreign office envelope.

TERMS WHICH RUSSIA OFFERED TO ACCEPT

As I said, I was sent to obtain an exact statement of the terms that the Soviet Government was ready to accept, and I received on the 14th the following statement from Tchitcherin and Litvinov.

Senator KNOX. Who were they?

Mr. BULLITT. Tchitcherin was Peoples' Commisar for Foreign Affairs of the Soviet Republic and Litvinov was the former Soviet Ambassador to London, the man with whom Buckler had had his conversation, and who was now practically assistant secretary for foreign affairs.

I also had a conference with Lenin. The Soviet Government undertook to accept this proposal provided it was made by the allied and associated Governments not later than April 10, 1919. The proposal reads as follows [reading]:

TEXT OF PROJECTED PEACE PROPOSAL BY THE ALLIED AND ASSOCIATED GOVERNMENTS.

The allied and associated Governments to propose that hostilities shall cease on all fronts in the territory of the former Russian Empire and Finland on ——[1] and that no new hostilities shall begin after this date, pending a conference to be held at ——[2] on ——[3]

[Footnote 1: The date of the armistice to be set at least a week after the date when the allied and associated Governments make this proposal.]

[Footnote 2: The Soviet Government greatly prefers that the conference should be held in a neutral country and also that either a radio or a direct telegraph wire to Moscow should be put at its disposal.]

[Footnote 3: The conference to begin not later than a week after the armistice takes effect and the Soviet Government greatly prefers that the period between the date of the armistice and the first meeting of the conference should be only three days, if possible.]

The duration of the armistice to be for two weeks, unless extended by mutual consent, and all parties to the armistice to undertake not to employ the period of the armistice to transfer troops and war material to the territory of the former Russian Empire.

The conference to discuss peace on the basis of the following principles, which shall not be subject to revision by the conference.

1. All existing de facto governments which have been set up on the territory of the former Russian Empire and Finland to remain in full control of the territories which they occupy at the moment when the armistice becomes effective, except in so far as the conference may agree upon the transfer of territories; until the peoples inhabiting the territories controlled by these de facto governments shall themselves determine to change their Governments. The Russian Soviet Government, the other soviet governments and all other governments which have been set up on the territory of the former Russian Empire, the allied and associated Governments, and the other

15

Governments which are operating against the soviet governments, including Finland, Poland, Galicia, Roumania, Armenia, Azerbaidjan, and Afghanistan, to agree not to attempt to upset by force the existing de facto governments which have been set up on the territory of the former Russian Empire and the other Governments signatory to this agreement. [Footnote 4: The allied and associated Governments to undertake to see to it that the de facto governments of Germany do not attempt to upset by force the de facto governments of Russia. The de facto governments which have been set up on the territory of the former Russian Empire to undertake not to attempt to upset by force the de facto governments of Germany.]

2. The economic blockade to be raised and trade relations between Soviet Russia and the allied and associated countries to be reestablished under conditions which will ensure that supplies from the allied and associated countries are made available on equal terms to all classes of the Russian people.

3. The soviet governments of Russia to have the right of unhindered transit on all railways and the use of all ports which belonged to the former Russian Empire and to Finland and are necessary for the disembarkation and transportation of passengers and goods between their territories and the sea; detailed arrangements for the carrying out of this provision to be agreed upon at the conference.

4. The citizens of the soviet republics of Russia to have the right of free entry into the allied and associated countries as well as into all countries which have been formed on the territory of the former Russian Empire and Finland; also the right of sojourn and of circulation and full security, provided they do not interfere in the domestic politics of those countries. [Footnote 5: It is considered essential by the Soviet Government that the allied and associated Governments should see to it that Poland and all neutral countries extend the same rights as the allied and associated countries.]

Nationals of the allied and associated countries and of the other countries above named to have the right of free entry into the soviet republics of Russia; also the right of sojourn and of circulation and full security, provided they do not interfere in the domestic politics of the soviet republics.

The allied and associated Governments and other governments which have been set up on the territory of the former Russian Empire and Finland to have the right to send official representatives enjoying full liberty and immunity into the various Russian Soviet Republics. The soviet governments of Russia to have the right to send official representatives enjoying full liberty and immunity into all the allied and associated countries and into the nonsoviet countries which have been formed on the territory of the former Russian Empire and Finland.

5. The soviet governments, the other Governments which have been set up on the territory of the former Russian Empire and Finland, to give a general amnesty to all political opponents, offenders, and prisoners. The allied and associated governments to give a general amnesty to all Russian political opponents, offenders, and prisoners, and to their own nationals who have been or may be prosecuted for giving help to Soviet Russia. All Russians who have fought in, or otherwise aided the armies opposed to the soviet governments, and those opposed to the other Governments which have been set up on the territory of the former Russian Empire and Finland to be included in this amnesty.

All prisoners of war of non-Russian powers detained in Russia, likewise all nationals of those powers now in Russia to be given full facilities for repatriation. The Russian prisoners of war in whatever foreign country they may be, likewise all Russian nationals, including the Russian soldiers and officers abroad and those serving in all foreign armies to be given full facilities for repatriation.

6. Immediately after the signing of this agreement all troops of the allied and associated Governments and other non-Russian Governments to be withdrawn from Russia and military assistance to cease to be given to antisoviet Governments which have been set up on the territory of the former Russian Empire.

The soviet governments and the antisoviet governments which have been set up on the territory of the former Russian Empire and Finland to begin to reduce their armies simultaneously, and at the same rate, to a peace footing immediately after the signing of this agreement. The conference to determine the most effective and just method of inspecting and controlling this simultaneous demobilization and also the withdrawal of the troops and the cessation of military assistance to the antisoviet governments.

7. The allied and associated Governments, taking cognizance of the statement of the Soviet Government of Russia, in its note of February 4, in regard to its foreign debts, propose as an integral part of this agreement that the soviet governments and the other governments which have been set up on the territory of the former Russian Empire and Finland shall recognize their responsibility for the financial obligations of the former Russian Empire, to foreign States parties to this agreement and to the nationals of such States. Detailed arrangements for the payment of these debts to be agreed upon at the conference, regard being had to the present financial position of Russia. The Russian gold seized by the Czecho-Slovaks in Kazan or taken from Germany by the Allies to be regarded as partial payment of the portion of the debt due from the soviet republics of Russia.

The Soviet Government of Russia undertakes to accept the foregoing proposal provided it is made not later than April 10, 1919.

In regard to the second sentence in paragraph 5, in regard to "giving help to Soviet Russia" I may say that I was told that that was not a sine qua non but it was necessary in order to get the proposal through the Russian executive committee, which it had to pass before it was handed to me. I was also handed an additional sheet, which I refused to take as a part of the formal document, containing the following:

The Soviet Government is most anxious to have a semiofficial guaranty from the American and British Governments that they will do their utmost to see to it that France lives up to the conditions of the armistice.

The Soviet Government had a deep suspicion of the French Government.

In reference to this matter, and in explanation of that proposal, I sent a number of telegrams from Helsingfors. I feel that in a way it is important, for an explanation of the matter, that those telegrams should be made public, but, on the other hand, they were sent in a confidential code of the Department of State, and I do not feel at liberty to read them unless ordered to specifically by the committee. I should not wish to take the responsibility for breaking a code which is in current use by the department.

Senator KNOX. I should think your scruples were well founded. I should not read those telegrams.

Mr. BULLITT. I can simply inform you briefly of the nature of them.

Senator KNOX. You might give us the nature of them. To whom were they sent?

Mr. BULLITT. On reaching Petrograd I sent Capt. Pettit out to Helsingfors after I had had a discussion with Tchitcherin and with Litvinov with a telegram, in which I said I had reached Petrograd and had perfected arrangements to cross the boundary at will, and to communicate with the mission via the consul at Helsingfors; that the journey had been easy, and that the reports of frightful conditions in Petrograd had been ridiculously exaggerated.

I described the discussions I had had with Tchitcherin and with Litvinov, and said they had assured me that after going to Moscow and after discussion with Lenin, I should be able to carry out a specific statement of the position of the Soviet Government on all points.

On reaching Helsingfors I sent a telegram to the mission at Paris "Most secret, for the President, Secretary Lansing, and Col. House only," in which I said that in handing me the statement which I have just read, Tchitcherin and Litvinov had explained that the Executive Council of the Soviet Government had formally considered and adopted it, and that the Soviet Government considered itself absolutely bound to accept the proposals made therein, provided they were made on or before April 10, and under no conditions would they change their minds.

I also explained that I had found Lenin, Tchitcherin, and Litvinov full of the sense of Russia's need for peace, and that I felt the details of their statement might be modified without making it unacceptable to them, and that in particular the clause under article 5 was not of vital importance. That, on the other hand, I felt that in the main this statement represented the minimum terms that the Soviet Government would accept.

I explained that it was understood with regard to article 2 that the allied and associated countries should have a right to send inspectors into Soviet Russia and see to it that the disposition of supplies, if the blockade was lifted, was entirely equitable, and I explained also that it was fully understood that the phrase under article 4 on "official representatives" did not include diplomatic representatives, that the Soviet Government simply desired to have some agents who might more or less look out for their people here.

I explained further that in regard to footnote No. 2, the Soviet Government hoped and preferred that the conference should be held in Norway; that its preferences thereafter were, first, some point in between Russia and Finland; second, a large ocean liner anchored off Moon Island or the Aland Islands; and, fourth, Prinkipos.

I also explained that Tchitcherin and all the other members of the government with whom I had talked had said in the most positive and unequivocal manner that the Soviet Government was determined to pay its foreign debts, and I was convinced that there would be no dispute on that point.

Senator KNOX. Do you know how these telegrams were received in Paris, whether favorably or unfavorably?

Mr. BULLITT. I can only say, in regard to that, there are three other very brief ones. One was on a subject which I might give you the gist of before I go on with it.

Senator KNOX. Go ahead, in your own way.

Mr. BULLITT. Col. House sent me a message of congratulation on receipt of them, and by one of the curious quirks of the conference, a member of the secretariat refused to send the message because of the way in which it was signed, and Col. House was only able to give me a copy of it when I reached Paris. I have a copy of it here.

Senator HARDING. Would not this story be more interesting if we knew which member of the conference objected?

Mr. BULLITT. I believe the objection was on the technical point that Col. House had signed "Ammission" instead of his name, but I really do not know which member of the conference it was that made the objection.

I then sent another telegram, which is rather long, too long to attempt to paraphrase, and I will ask that I may not put it in, because the entire substance of it is contained in briefer form in my formal report. This telegram itself is in code.

Senator BRANDEGEE. Are there any translations of those of your telegrams that are in code?

Mr. BULLITT. No; I have given you the substance of them as I have gone along.

As I said to you before, Secretary Lansing had instructed me if possible to obtain the release of Mr. Treadwell, our consul at Tashkent, somewhere between 4,000 and 5,000 miles from Moscow. In Moscow I had spoken to Lenin and Tchitcherin and Litvinov in regard to it, and finally they said they recognized that it was foolish to hold him; that they had never really given much thought to the matter; that he had been held by the local government at Tashkent, which was more than 4,000 miles away; that raids were being made on the railroad constantly, and they might have some difficulty in communicating. However, they promised me that they would send a telegram at once ordering his release, and that they would send him out either by Persia or by Finland whichever way he preferred. I told them I was sure he would prefer to go by way of Finland. Here is a copy of their telegram ordering his release, which will not be of much use to you, I fear, as it is in Russian. They carried out this promise to the letter, releasing Treadwell at once, and Treadwell in due course of time and in good health appeared on the frontier of Finland on the 27th of April. All that time was consumed in travel from Tashkent, which is a long way under present conditions.

Senator NEW. I saw Mr. Treadwell here some time ago.

Mr. BULLITT. I then sent a telegram in regard to Mr. Pettit, the officer of military intelligence, who was with me as my assistant, saying I intended to send him back to Petrograd at once to keep in touch with the situation so that we should have information constantly. I will say in this connection that it was not an extraordinary thing for the various Governments to have representatives in Russia. The British Government had a man in there at the same time that I was there. He was traveling as a Red Cross representative, but in reality he was there for the Foreign Office, a Maj. A.R. Parker, I believe. I am not certain of his name, but we can verify it.

I also sent a telegram from Helsingfors, "strictly personal to Col. House," requesting him to show my fifth and sixth telegrams to Mr. Philip Kerr, Mr. Lloyd George's secretary, so that Mr.

Lloyd George might be at once informed in regard to the situation, inasmuch as he had known I was going, and inasmuch as the British had been so courteous as to offer to send me across on a cruiser. When I got to London and found that the torpedo boat on which I had expected to go was escorting the President, Mr. Lloyd George's office in London called up the Admiralty and asked them to give me a boat in which to go across. Incidentally I was informed by Col. House, on my arrival in Paris, that copies of my telegrams had been sent at once to Mr. Lloyd George and Mr. Balfour.

Senator KNOX. Mr. Bullitt, I do not think we need to go into quite so much detail. You have told us now with what instructions you went, what the British attitude was, what the American attitude was, and what the Soviet Government proposed. Now, let us have your report.

Mr. BULLITT. All right, sir. This was my report—

Senator BRANDEGEE. What is the date of that, please?

Mr. BULLITT. This copy does not bear the date on it. On the other hand I can tell you within a day or two. The date unfortunately was left off of this particular copy. It was made on or about the 27th or 28th day of March, in the week before April 1.

Senator BRANDEGEE. 1919?

Mr. BULLITT. 1919. I unquestionably could obtain from Secretary Lansing or the President or some one else the actual original of the report.

Senator BRANDEGEE. I do not care about the precise date, but I want to get it approximately.

Mr. BULLITT. It was about the 1st day of April.

Senator KNOX. To whom was the report made?

Mr. BULLITT. The report was addressed to the President and the American Commissioners Plenipotentiary to Negotiate Peace. I was ordered to make it. I had sent all these telegrams from Helsingfors, and I felt personally that no report was necessary, but the President desired a written report, and I made the report as follows:

MR. BULLITT'S REPORT ON RUSSIA
ECONOMIC SITUATION

Russia to-day is in a condition of acute economic distress. The blockade by land and sea is the cause of this distress and lack of the essentials of transportation is its gravest symptom. Only one-fourth of the locomotives which ran on Russian lines before the war are now available for use. Furthermore, Soviet Russia is cut off entirely from all supplies of coal and gasoline. In consequence, transportation by all steam and electric vehicles is greatly hampered; and transportation by automobile and by the fleet of gasoline-using Volga steamers and canal boats is impossible. (Appendix, p. 55.)

As a result of these hindrances to transportation it is possible to bring from the grain centers to Moscow only 25 carloads of food a day, instead of the 100 carloads which are essential, and to Petrograd only 15 carloads, instead of the essential 50. In consequence, every man, woman, and child in Moscow and Petrograd is suffering from slow starvation. (Appendix, p. 56.)

Mortality is particularly high among new-born children whose mothers can not suckle them, among newly-delivered mothers, and among the aged. The entire population, in addition, is exceptionally susceptible to disease; and a slight illness is apt to result fatally because of the total lack of medicines. Typhoid, typhus, and smallpox are epidemic in both Petrograd and Moscow.

Industry, except the production of munitions of war, is largely at a standstill. Nearly all means of transport which are not employed in carrying food are used to supply the army, and there is scarcely any surplus transport to carry materials essential to normal industry. Furthermore, the army has absorbed the best executive brains and physical vigor of the nation. In addition, Soviet Russia is cut off from most of its sources of iron and of cotton. Only the flax, hemp, wood, and lumber industries have an adequate supply of raw material.

On the other hand, such essentials of economic life as are available are being utilized to the utmost by the Soviet Government. Such trains as there are, run on time. The distribution of food is well controlled. Many industrial experts of the old régime are again managing their plants and sabotage by such managers has ceased. Loafing by the workmen during work hours has been overcome. (Appendix, p. 57.)

SOCIAL CONDITIONS

19

The destructive phase of the revolution is over and all the energy of the Government is turned to constructive work. The terror has ceased. All power of judgment has been taken away from the extraordinary commission for suppression of the counter-revolution, which now merely accuses suspected counter-revolutionaries, who are tried by the regular, established, legal tribunals. Executions are extremely rare. Good order has been established. The streets are safe. Shooting has ceased. There are few robberies. Prostitution has disappeared from sight. Family life has been unchanged by the revolution, the canard in regard to "nationalization of women" notwithstanding. (Appendix, p. 58.)

The theaters, opera, and ballet are performing as in peace. Thousands of new schools have been opened in all parts of Russia and the Soviet Government seems to have done more for the education of the Russian people in a year and a half than czardom did in 50 years. (Appendix, p. 59.)

POLITICAL SITUATION

The Soviet form of government is firmly established. Perhaps the most striking fact in Russia today is the general support which is given the government by the people in spite of their starvation. Indeed, the people lay the blame for their distress wholly on the blockade and on the governments which maintain it. The Soviet form of government seems to have become to the Russian people the symbol of their revolution. Unquestionably it is a form of government which lends itself to gross abuse and tyranny but it meets the demand of the moment in Russia and it has acquired so great a hold on the imagination of the common people that the women are ready to starve and the young men to die for it.

The position of the communist party (formerly Bolsheviki) is also very strong. Blockade and intervention have caused the chief opposition parties, the right social revolutionaries and the menshiviki, to give temporary support to the communists. These opposition parties have both made formal statements against the blockade, intervention, and the support of antisoviet governments by the allied and associated governments. Their leaders, Volsky and Martov, are most vigorous in their demands for the immediate raising of the blockade and peace. (Appendix, p. 60.)

Indeed, the only ponderable opposition to the communists to-day comes from more radical parties—the left social revolutionaries and the anarchists. These parties, in published statements, call the communists, and particularly Lenin and Tchitcherin, "the paid bourgeois gendarmes of the Entente." They attack the communists because the communists have encouraged scientists, engineers, and industrial experts of the bourgeois class to take important posts under the Soviet Government at high pay. They rage against the employment of bourgeois officers in the army and against the efforts of the communists to obtain peace. They demand the immediate massacre of all the bourgeoisie and an immediate declaration of war on all nonrevolutionary governments. They argue that the Entente Governments should be forced to intervene more deeply in Russia, asserting that such action would surely provoke the proletariat of all European countries to immediate revolution.

Within the communist party itself there is a distinct division of opinion in regard to foreign policy, but this disagreement has not developed personal hostility or open breach in the ranks of the party. Trotski, the generals, and many theorists believe the red army should go forward everywhere until more vigorous intervention by the Entente is provoked, which they, too, count upon to bring revolution in France and England. Their attitude is not a little colored by pride in the spirited young army. (Appendix, p. 62.) Lenin, Tchitcherin, and the bulk of the communist party, on the other hand, insist that the essential problem at present is to save the proletariat of Russia, in particular, and the proletariat of Europe, in general, from starvation, and assert that it will benefit the revolution but little to conquer all Europe if the Government of the United States replies by starving all Europe. They advocate, therefore, the conciliation of the United States even at the cost of compromising with many of the principles they hold most dear. And Lenin's prestige in Russia at present is so overwhelming that the Trotski group is forced reluctantly to follow him. (Appendix, p. 63.)

Lenin, indeed, as a practical matter, stands well to the right in the existing political life of Russia. He recognizes the undesirability, from the Socialist viewpoint, of the compromises he feels compelled to make; but he is ready to make the compromises. Among the more notable concessions he has already made are: The abandonment of his plan to nationalize the land and the adoption of the policy of dividing it among the peasants, the establishment of savings banks paying 3 per cent interest, the decision to pay all foreign debts, and the decision to give concessions it that shall prove to be necessary to obtain credit abroad. (Appendix, p. 64.)

In a word, Lenin feels compelled to retreat from his theoretical position all along the line. He is ready to meet the western Governments half way.

PEACE PROPOSALS

Lenin seized upon the opportunity presented by my trip of investigation to make a definite statement of the position of the Soviet Government. He was opposed by Trotski and the generals, but without much difficulty got the support of the majority of the executive council, and the statement of the position of the Soviet Government which was handed to me was finally adopted unanimously.

My discussion of this proposal with the leaders of the Soviet Government was so detailed that I feel sure of my ground in saying that it does not represent the minimum terms of the Soviet Government, and that I can point out in detail wherein it may be modified without making it unacceptable to the Soviet Government. For example, the clause under article 5—"and to their own nationals who have been or may be prosecuted for giving help to Soviet Russia"—is certainly not of vital importance. And the clause under article 4, in regard to admission of citizens of the soviet republics of Russia into the allied and associated countries, may certainly be changed in such a way as to reserve all necessary rights to control such immigration to the allied and associated countries, and to confine it to persons who come on legitimate and necessary business, and to exclude definitely all possibility of an influx of propagandists.

CONCLUSIONS

The following conclusions are respectfully submitted:

1. No government save a socialist government can be set up in Russia to-day except by foreign bayonets, and any governments so set up will fall the moment such support is withdrawn. The Lenin wing of the communist party is to-day as moderate as any socialist government which can control Russia.

2. No real peace can be established in Europe or the world until peace is made with the revolution. This proposal of the Soviet Government presents an opportunity to make peace with the revolution on a just and reasonable basis—perhaps a unique opportunity.

3. If the blockade is lifted and supplies begin to be delivered regularly to soviet Russia, a more powerful hold over the Russian people will be established than that given by the blockade itself—the hold given by fear that this delivery of supplies may be stopped. Furthermore, the parties which oppose the communists in principle but are supporting them at present will be able to begin to fight against them.

4. It is, therefore, respectfully recommended that a proposal following the general lines of the suggestion of the Soviet Government should be made at the earliest possible moment, such changes being made, particularly in article 4 and article 5, as will make the proposal acceptable to conservative opinion in the allied and associated countries.

Very respectfully submitted.
WILLIAM C. BULLITT.
* * * * *

APPENDIX TO REPORT
TRANSPORT

Locomotives.—Before the war Russia had 22,000 locomotives. Destruction by war and ordinary wear and tear have reduced the number of locomotives in good order to 5,500. Russia is entirely cut off from supplies of spare parts and materials for repair, facilities for the manufacture of which do not exist in Russia. And the Soviet Government is able only with the greatest difficulty to keep in running order the few locomotives at its disposal.

Coal.—Soviet Russia is entirely cut off from supplies of coal. Kolchak holds the Perm mining district, although Soviet troops are now on the edge of it. Denikin still holds the larger part of the Donetz coal district and has destroyed the mines in the portion of the district which he has evacuated. As a result of this, locomotives, electrical power plants, etc., must be fed with wood, which is enormously expensive and laborious and comparatively ineffectual.

Gasoline.—There is a total lack of gasoline, due to the British occupation of Baku. The few automobiles in the cities which are kept running for vital Government business are fed with substitute mixtures, which causes them to break down with great frequency and to miss continually. Almost the entire fleet on the great inland waterway system of Russia was propelled by gasoline. As a result the Volga and the canals, which are so vital a part of Russia's system of transportation, are useless.

FOOD

Everyone is hungry in Moscow and Petrograd, including the people's commissaries themselves. The daily ration of Lenin and the other commissaries is the same as that of a soldier in the army or of a workman at hard labor. In the hotel which is reserved for Government officials the menu is the following: Breakfast—A quarter to half a pound of black bread, which must last all day, and tea without sugar. Dinner—A good soup, a small piece of fish, for which occasionally a diminutive piece of meat is substituted, a vegetable, either a potato or a bit of cabbage, more tea without sugar. Supper—What remains of the morning ration of bread and more tea without sugar.

Occasionally sugar, butter, and chickens slip through from the Ukraine and are sold secretly at atrocious prices—butter, for example, at 140 roubles a pound. Whenever the Government is able to get its hands on any such "luxuries" it turns them over to the schools, where an attempt is made to give every child a good dinner every day.

The food situation has been slightly improved by the rejoining of Ukraine to Great Russia, for food is relatively plentiful in the south; but no great improvement in the situation is possible because of the lack of transport.

MANAGEMENT

Such supplies as are available in Soviet Russia are being utilized with considerable skill. For example, in spite of the necessity of firing with wood, the Moscow-Petrograd express keeps up to its schedule, and on both occasions when I made the trip it took but 13 hours, compared to the 12 hours of prewar days.

The food control works well, so that there is no abundance alongside of famine. Powerful and weak alike endure about the same degree of starvation.

The Soviet Government has made great efforts to persuade industrial managers and technical experts of the old régime to enter its service. Many very prominent men have done so. And the Soviet Government pays them as high as $45,000 a year for their services, although Lenin gets but $1,800 a year. This very anomalous situation arises from the principle that any believing communist must adhere to the scale of wages established by the government, but if the government considers it necessary to have the assistance of any anticommunist, it is permitted to pay him as much as he demands.

All meetings of workmen during work hours have been prohibited, with the result that the loafing which was so fatal during the Kerensky régime has been overcome and discipline has been restored in the factories as in the army.

SOCIAL CONDITIONS

Terror.—The red terror is over. During the period of its power the extraordinary commission for the suppression of the counter revolution, which was the instrument of the terror, executed about 1,500 persons in Petrograd, 500 in Moscow, and 3,000 in the remainder of the country— 5,000 in all Russia. These figures agree with those which were brought back from Russia by Maj. Wardwell, and inasmuch as I have checked them from Soviet, anti-Soviet, and neutral sources I believe them to be approximately correct. It is worthy of note in this connection that in the white terror in southern Finland alone, according to official figures, Gen. Mannerheim executed without trial 12,000 working men and women.

Order.—One feels as safe in the streets of Petrograd and Moscow as in the streets of Paris or New York. On the other hand, the streets of these cities are dismal, because of the closing of retail shops whose functions are now concentrated in a few large nationalized "department stores." Petrograd, furthermore, has been deserted by half its population; but Moscow teems with twice the number of inhabitants it contained before the war. The only noticeable difference in the theaters, opera, and ballet is that they are now run under the direction of the department of education, which prefers classics and sees to it that working men and women and children are given an opportunity to attend the performances and that they are instructed beforehand in the significance and beauties of the productions.

Morals.—Prostitutes have disappeared from sight, the economic reasons for their career having ceased to exist. Family life has been absolutely unchanged by the revolution. I have never heard more genuinely mirthful laughter than when I told Lenin, Tchitcherin, and Litvinov that much of the world believed that women had been "nationalized." This lie is so wildly fantastic that they will not even take the trouble to deny it. Respect for womanhood was never greater than in Russia to-day. Indeed, the day I reached Petrograd was a holiday in honor of wives and mothers.

Education.—The achievements of the department of education under Lunacharsky have been very great. Not only have all the Russian classics been reprinted in editions of three and five million copies and sold at a low price to the people, but thousands of new schools for men, women, and children have been opened in all parts of Russia. Furthermore, workingmen's and soldiers' clubs have been organized in many of the palaces of yesteryear, where the people are instructed by means of moving pictures and lectures. In the art galleries one meets classes of working men and women being instructed in the beauties of the pictures. The children's schools have been entirely reorganized, and an attempt is being made to give every child a good dinner at school every day. Furthermore, very remarkable schools have been opened for defective and over-nervous children. On the theory that genius and insanity are closely allied, these children are taught from the first to compose music, paint pictures, sculpt and write poetry, and it is asserted that some very valuable results have been achieved, not only in the way of productions but also in the way of restoring the nervous systems of the children.

Morale.—The belief of the convinced communists in their cause is almost religious. Never in any religious service have I seen higher emotional unity than prevailed at the meeting of the Petrograd Soviet in celebration of the foundation of the Third Socialist Internationale. The remark of one young man to me when I questioned him in regard to his starved appearance is characteristic. He replied very simply: "I am ready to give another year of starvation to our revolution."

STATEMENTS OF LEADERS OF OPPOSITION PARTIES

The following statement was made to me by Volsky, leader of the right social revolutionaries, the largest opposition party:

"Intervention of any kind will prolong the régime of the Bolsheviki by compelling us, like all honorable Russians, to drop opposition and rally round the Soviet Government in defense of the revolution. With regard to help to individual groups or governments fighting against soviet Russia, we see no difference between such intervention and the sending of troops. If the allies come to an agreement with the Soviet Government, sooner or later the peasant masses will make their will felt and they are alike against the bourgeoisie and the Bolsheviki.

"If by any chance Kolchak and Denikin were to win, they would have to kill in tens of thousands where the Bolsheviki have had to kill in hundreds and the result would be the complete ruin and collapse of Russia into anarchy. Has not the Ukraine been enough to teach the allies that occupation by non-Bolshevik troops merely turns into Bolsheviki those of the population who were not Bolsheviki before? It is clear to us that the Bolshiviki are really fighting against bourgeois dictatorship, We are, therefore, prepared to help them in every possible way.

"Grandmother Ekaterina Constantinovna Breshkovskaya has no sort of authority, either from the assembly of members of the all Russian constituent assembly or from the party of social revolutionaries. Her utterances in America, if she is preaching intervention, represent her personal opinions which are categorically repudiated by the party of social revolutionaries, which has decisively expressed itself against the permissibility of intervention, direct or indirect."

Volsky signed this latter statement: "V. Volsky, late president of the assembly of members of the all Russian constituent assembly."

Martov, leader of the Menshiviki, stated: "The Menshiviki are against every form of intervention, direct or indirect, because by providing the incentive to militarization it is bound to emphasize the least desirable qualities of the revolution. Further, the needs of the army overwhelm all efforts at meeting the needs of social and economic reconstruction. Agreement with the Soviet Government would lessen the tension of defense and would unmuzzle the opposition, who, while the Soviet Government is attacked, are prepared to help in its defense, while reserving until peace their efforts to alter the Bolshevik régime.

"The forces that would support intervention must be dominated by those of extreme reaction because all but the reactionaries are prepared temporarily to sink their differences with the Bolsheviki in order to defend the revolution as a whole."

Martov finally expressed himself as convinced that, given peace, life itself and the needs of the country will bring about the changes he desires.

ARMY

The soviet army now numbers between 1,000,000 and 1,200,000 troops of the line. Nearly all these soldiers are young men between the ages of 17 and 27. The morale of regiments varies greatly. The convinced communists, who compose the bulk of the army, fight with crusading enthusiasm. Other regiments, composed of patriots but noncommunists, are less spirited; other regiments composed of men who have entered the army for the slightly higher bread ration are distinctly untrustworthy. Great numbers of officers of the old army are occupying important executive posts in the administration of the new army, but are under control of convinced communist supervisors. Nearly all the lower grade officers of the army are workmen who have displayed courage in the ranks and have been trained in special officer schools. Discipline has been restored and on the whole the spirit of the army appears to be very high, particularly since its recent successes. The soldiers no longer have the beaten dog-like look which distinguished them under the Czar but carry themselves like freemen and curiously like Americans. They are popular with the people.

I witnessed a review of 15,000 troops in Petrograd. The men marched well and their equipment of shoes, uniforms, rifles, and machine guns and light artillery was excellent. On the other hand they have no big guns, no aeroplanes, no gas shells, no liquid fire, nor indeed, any of the more refined instruments of destruction.

The testimony was universal that recruiting for the army is easiest in the districts which having once lived under the soviet were over run by anti-soviet forces and then reoccupied by the Red Army.

Trotski is enormously proud of the army he has created, but it is noteworthy that even he is ready to disband the army at once if peace can be obtained in order that all the brains and energy it contains may be turned to restoring the normal life of the country.

LENIN'S PRESTIGE

The hold which Lenin has gained on the imagination of the Russian people makes his position almost that of a dictator. There is already a Lenin legend. He is regarded as almost a prophet. His picture, usually accompanied by that of Karl Marx, hangs everywhere. In Russia one never hears Lenin and Trotski spoken of in the same breath as is usual in the western world. Lenin is regarded as in a class by himself. Trotski is but one of the lower order of mortals.

When I called on Lenin at the Kremlin I had to wait a few minutes until a delegation of peasants left his room. They had heard in their village that Comrade Lenin was hungry. And they had come hundreds of miles carrying 800 poods of bread as the gift of the village to Lenin. Just before them was another delegation of peasants to whom the report had come that Comrade Lenin was working in an unheated room. They came bearing a stove and enough firewood to heat it for three months. Lenin is the only leader who receives such gifts. And he turns them into the common fund.

Face to face Lenin is a very striking man—straightforward and direct, but also genial and with a large humor and serenity.

CONCESSIONS

The Soviet Government recognizes very clearly the undesirability of granting concessions to foreigners and is ready to do so only because of necessity. The members of the Government realize that the lifting of the blockade will be illusory unless the Soviet Government is able to establish credits in foreign countries, particularly the United States and England, so that goods may be bought in those countries. For Russia to-day is in a position to export only a little gold, a little platinum, a little hemp, flax, and wood. These exports will be utterly inadequate to pay for the vast quantity of imports which Russia needs. Russia must, therefore, obtain credit at any price. The members of the Soviet Government realize fully that as a preliminary step to the obtaining of credit the payment of foreign debts must be resumed and, therefore, are ready to pay such debts. But even though these debts are paid the members of the Soviet Government believe that they will not be able to borrow money in foreign countries on any mere promise to pay. They believe, therefore, that they will have to grant concessions in Russia to foreigners in order to obtain immediate credit. They desire to avoid this expedient if in any way it shall be possible, but if absolutely necessary they are ready to adopt it in order to begin the restoration of the normal life of the country.

Senator KNOX. To whom did you hand that report?

Mr. BULLITT. I handed copies of this personally to Secretary Lansing, Col. House, Gen. Bliss and Mr. Henry White, and I handed a second copy, for the President, to Mr. Lansing. Secretary Lansing wrote on it, "Urgent and immediate"; put it in an envelope, and I took it up to the President's house.

Senator KNOX. At the same time that you handed in this report, did you hand them the proposal of the Soviet Government?

Mr. BULLITT. The proposal of the Soviet Government is appended to this report.

Senator KNOX. It is a part of the report?

Mr. BULLITT. It is a part of the report which I have already read. There comes first an appendix explaining the statements which I have just read, and giving the evidence I have for them.

Senator KNOX. Was there any formal meeting of the peace conference, or of representatives of the great powers, to act upon this suggestion and upon your report?

Mr. BULLITT. It was acted upon in a very lengthy, long-drawn-out manner.

Immediately on my return I was first asked to appear before the American Commission. First, the night I got back I had a couple of hours with Col. House, in which I went over the whole matter. Col. House was entirely and quite decidedly in favor of making peace, if possible, on the basis of this proposal.

The next morning I was called before the other Commissioners, and I talked with Mr. Lansing, Gen. Bliss, and Mr. Henry White all the morning and most of the afternoon. We had a long discussion, at the end of which it was the sense of the commissioners' meeting that it was highly desirable to attempt to bring about peace on that basis.

BREAKFAST WITH LLOYD GEORGE

The next morning I had breakfast with Mr. Lloyd George at his apartment. Gen. Smuts and Sir Maurice Hankey and Mr. Philip Kerr were also present, and we discussed the matter at considerable length, I brought Mr. Lloyd George the official text of the proposal, the same official one, in that same envelop, which I have just shown to you. He had previously read it, it having been telegraphed from Helsingfors. As he had previously read it, he merely glanced over it and said, "That is the same one I have already read," and he handed it to Gen. Smuts, who was across the table, and said, "General, this is of the utmost importance and interest, and you ought to read it right away." Gen. Smuts read it immediately, and said he thought it should not be allowed to lapse; that it was of the utmost importance. Mr. Lloyd George, however, said that he did not know what he could do with British public opinion. He had a copy of the Daily Mail in his hand, and he said, "As long as the British press is doing this kind of thing how can you expect me to be sensible about Russia?" The Daily Mail was roaring and screaming about the whole Russian situation. Then Mr. Lloyd George said, "Of course all the reports we get from people we send in there are in this same general direction, but we have got to send in somebody who is known to the whole world as a complete conservative, in order to have the whole world believe that the report he brings out is not simply the utterance of a radical." He then said, "I wonder if we could get Lansdowne to go?" Then he immediately corrected himself and said, "No; it would probably kill him." Then he said, "I wish I could send Bob Cecil, but we have got to keep him for the league of nations." And he said to Smuts, "It would be splendid if you could go, but, of course, you have got the other job," which was going down to Hungary. Afterwards he said he thought the most desirable man to send was the Marquis of Salisbury, Lord Robert Cecil's brother; that he would be respectable enough and well known enough so that when he came back and made the same report it would go down with British public opinion. Mr. Lloyd George then urged me to make public my report. He said it was absolutely necessary to have publicity given to the actual conditions in Russia, which he recognized were as presented.

I saw Mr. Balfour that afternoon with Sir Eric Drummond, who at that time was acting as his secretary. He is now secretary of the league of nations. We discussed the entire matter. Sir William Wiseman told me afterward that Mr. Balfour was thoroughly in favor of the proposition.

Well, to cut the story short, first the President referred the matter to Col. House. He left his decision on the matter with Col. House, as was his usual course of procedure in most such matters. Mr. Lloyd George also agreed in advance to leave the preparation of the proposal to Col. House; that is, he said he would be disposed to go at least as far as we would and would follow the lead of the President and Col. House. Col. House thereupon asked me to prepare a reply to this proposal, which I did.

Col. House in the meantime had seen Mr. Orlando, and Mr. Orlando had expressed himself as entirely in favor of making peace on this basis, at least so Col. House informed me at the time. The French, I believe, had not yet been approached formally on the matter.

Senator KNOX. By the way, right here, you say Mr. Lloyd George advised you to make your report public. Did you make it public?

Mr. BULLITT. No, sir. Mr. Lloyd George desired me to make it public for the enlightenment that he thought it might give to public opinion.

Senator KNOX. But you did not do it?

BULLITT REPORT SUPPRESSED

Mr. BULLITT. I attempted to. I prepared a statement for the press based on my report, giving the facts, which I submitted to the commission to be given out. No member of the commission was ready to take the responsibility for publicity in the matter and it was referred to the President. The President received it and decided that he did not want it given out. He thought he would rather keep it secret, and in spite of the urgings of the other commissioners he continued to adhere to that point of view, and my report has never been made public until this moment.

Col. House asked me to prepare a declaration of policy, a statement based on this proposal of the Soviet Government. It was to be an ironclad declaration which we knew in advance would be accepted by the Soviet Government if we made it, and he thought that the President and Mr. Lloyd George would put it through.

Senator BRANDEGEE. Did you attend that meeting of the commission when that report was considered by the American Commission?

Mr. BULLITT. I first handed each member of the commission my report. I had appeared before them and discussed my mission for an entire day. They sat in the morning and in the afternoon.

Senator BRANDEGEE. I wondered whether you were present when the President thought it would be better not to give it out, not to make it public.

Mr. BULLITT. No, sir; I was not. Then upon order of Col. House, to whom the matter had been referred, I prepared this declaration of policy. I prepared it in conjunction with Mr. Whitney Shepherdson, who was Col. House's assistant secretary, and also versed in international law. I do not know that this is of any importance, aside from the fact that it is almost the only direct proposition to accept their proposal which was prepared. Col. House took this and held it under advisement and discussed it, I believe, with the President and other persons.

The CHAIRMAN. It had better be printed.

The document referred to is as follows:

A PROPOSED DECLARATION OF POLICY TO BE ISSUED IN THE NAME OF THE ASSOCIATED GOVERNMENTS AND AN OFFER OF AN ARMISTICE

The representatives of the States assembled in conference at Paris recently extended an invitation to the organized groups in Russia to lay down their arms and to send delegates to Prince's Island. These delegates were asked to "confer with the representatives of the associated powers in the freest and frankest way, with a view to ascertaining the wishes of all sections of the Russian people and bringing about, if possible, some understanding and agreement by which Russia may work out her own purposes and happy cooperative relations may be established between her people and the other peoples of the world." The truce of arms was not declared, and the meeting did not take place.

The people of Russia are laboring to-day to establish the system of government under which they shall live. Their task is one of unparalleled difficulty, and should not be further complicated by

26

the existence of misapprehensions among the Russian people or throughout the world. Therefore, the representatives of the associated powers, now sitting in the conference of Paris, have determined to state publicly what they had in mind to say through their delegates to Prince's Island concerning the policies which govern their relations with the Russian people.

They wish to make it plain that they do not intend to interfere in any way with the solution of the political, social, or economic problems of Russia. They believe that the peace of the world will largely depend upon a right settlement of these matters; but they equally recognize that any right settlement must proceed from the Russian people themselves, unembarrassed by influence or direction from without. On the other hand, the associated powers desired to have it clearly understood that they can have no dealings with any Russian Government which shall invade the territory of its neighbors or seek to impose its will upon other peoples by force. The full authority and military power of the associated governments will stand in the way of any such attempt.

The task of creating a stable government demands all the great strength of Russia, healed of the famine, misery, and disease which attend and delay the reconstruction. The associated powers have solemnly pledged their resources to relieve the stricken regions of Europe. Their efforts, begun in Belgium and in northern France during the course of the war, now extend to exhausted peoples from Finland to the Dalmatian coast. Ports long idle are busy again. Trainloads of food are moved into the interior and there are distributed with an impartial hand. Industry is awakened, and life is resumed at the point where it was broken off by war. These measures of relief will be continued until peace is signed and until nations are once more able to provide for their needs through the normal channels of commerce.

It is the earnest desire of the associated peoples similarly to assuage the distress of millions of men and women in Russia and to provide them with such physical conditions as will make life possible and desirable. Relief can not be effectively rendered, however, except by the employment of all available transportation facilities and the active cooperation of those exercising authority within the country.

These requisites can not be assured while Russia is still at war.

The allied and associated governments, therefore, propose an agreement between themselves and all governments now exercising political authority within the territory of the former Russian Empire, including Finland, together with Poland, Galicia, Roumania, Armenia, Azerbaidjan, and Afghanistan, that hostilities against one another shall cease on all fronts within these territories on April —— at noon; that fresh hostilities shall not be begun during the period of this armistice, and that no troops or war material of any kind whatever shall be transferred to or within these territories so long as the armistice shall continue. The duration of the armistice shall be for two weeks, unless extended by mutual consent. The allied and associated Governments propose that such of these Governments as are willing to accept the terms of this armistice shall send not more than three representatives each, together with necessary technical experts, to —— where they shall meet on April —— with representatives of the allied and associated Governments in conference to discuss peace, upon the basis of the following principles:

(1) All signatory Governments shall remain, as against each other, in full control of the territories which they occupy at the moment when the armistice becomes effective; subject only to such rectifications as may be agreed upon by the conference, or until the peoples inhabiting these territories shall themselves voluntarily determine to change their Government.

(2) The right of free entry, sojourn, circulation, and full security shall be accorded by the several signatories to the citizens of each other; provided, however, that such persons comply with the laws of the country to which they seek admittance, and provided also that they do not interfere or attempt to interfere in any way with the domestic politics of that country.

(3) The right to send official representatives enjoying full liberty and immunity shall be accorded by the several signatories to each other.

(4) A general amnesty shall be granted by the various signatories to all political or military opponents, offenders, and prisoners who are so regarded because of their association or affiliation with another signatory, provided that they have not otherwise violated the laws of the land.

(5) Nationals of one signatory residing or detained in the country of another shall be given all possible facilities for repatriation.

(6) The allied and associated Governments shall immediately withdraw their armed forces and further military support from the territory of the former Russian Empire, including Finland, and the various Governments within that territory shall effect a simultaneous reduction of armed forces according to a scheme of demobilization and control to be agreed upon by the conference.

(7) Any economic blockade imposed by one signatory as against another shall be lifted and trade relations shall be established, subject to a program of equitable distribution of supplies and utilization of transport facilities to be agreed upon by the conference.

(8) Provision shall be made by the conference for a mutual exchange of transit and port privileges among the several signatories.

(9) The conference shall be competent to discuss and determine any other matter which bears upon the problem of establishing peace within the territory of the former Russian Empire, including Finland, and the reestablishment of international relations among the signatories.

NOTE.—If it is desirable to include a specific reference to Russia's financial obligations, the following clause (8 bis) would be acceptable to the Soviet Government at least: "The governments which have been set up on the territory of the former Russian Empire and Finland shall recognize their responsibility for the financial obligations of the former Russian Empire to foreign States parties to this agreement and to the nationals of such States. Detailed arrangements for discharging these obligations shall be agreed upon by the conference, regard being had to the present financial situation of Russia."

Senator BRANDEGEE. Was this brought to the attention of the President?

Mr. BULLITT. The first night after I got in Col. House went to the telephone and called up the President right away and told him that I was in, and that he thought this was a matter of the utmost importance, and that it would seem to be an opportunity to make peace in a section of the world where there was no peace; in fact, where there were 23 wars. The President said he would see me the next evening down at Col. House's office, as I remember it. The next evening, however, the President had a headache and he did not come. The following afternoon Col. House said to me that he had seen the President and the President had said he had a one-track mind and was occupied with Germany at present, and he could not think about Russia, and that he had left the Russian matter all to him, Col. House. Therefore I continued to deal with Col. House directly on it inasmuch as he was the delegate of the President, and Lloyd George, in the matter. I used to see Col. House every day, indeed two or three times a day, on the subject, urging him to obtain action before April 10, which, as you will recall, was the date when this proposal was to expire.

NANSEN PLAN TO FEED RUSSIA

Meanwhile Mr. Hoover and Mr. Auchincloss had the idea of approaching peace with Russia by a feeding proposition, and they had approached Mr. Fridjof Nansen, the Arctic explorer, and got him to write and send the following letter to the President. You doubtless have seen his letter to the President.

PARIS, April 3, 1919.

MY DEAR MR. PRESIDENT: The present food situation in Russia, where hundreds of thousands of people are dying monthly from sheer starvation and disease, is one of the problems now uppermost in all men's minds. As it appears that no solution of this food and disease question has so far been reached in any direction, I would like to make a suggestion from a neutral point of view for the alleviation of this gigantic misery on purely humanitarian grounds.

It would appear to me possible to organize a purely humanitarian commission for the provisioning of Russia, the foodstuffs and medical supplies to be paid for, perhaps, to some considerable extent by Russia itself, the justice of distribution to be guaranteed by such a commission, the membership of the commission to be comprised of Norwegian, Swedish, and possibly Dutch, Danish, and Swiss nationalities. It does not appear that the existing authorities in Russia would refuse the intervention of such a commission of wholly nonpolitical order, devoted solely to the humanitarian purpose of saving life. If thus organized upon the lines of the Belgian Relief Commission, it would raise no question of political recognition or negotiations between the Allies with the existing authorities in Russia.

I recognize keenly the large political issues involved, and
I would be glad to know under what conditions you would
approve such an enterprise and whether such commission could

look for actual support in finance, shipping, and food and
medical supplies from the United States Government.

I am addressing a similar note to Messrs. Orlando,
Clemenceau, and Lloyd George. Believe me, my dear Mr.
President,

Yours, most respectfully,
FRIDJOF NANSEN.
His Excellency the PRESIDENT,
11 Place des Etats-Unis, Paris.

Senator KNOX, I think that was published in nearly all the papers.

Mr. BULLITT. Yes. In it he proposed that a commission should be formed at once for the
feeding of Russia, because of the frightful conditions of starvation and so on. Col. House decided
that it would be an easier way to peace if we could get there via the feeding plan, under the guise of
a purely humanitarian plan, if we could slide in that way instead of by a direct, outright statement
inviting these people to sit down and make peace. Therefore he asked me to prepare a reply to the
Nansen letter, which I have here.

PARIS, FRANCE, April 4, 1919. Suggested reply to Dr. Nansen by the President of the
United States and the premiers of France, Great Britain, and Italy:

DEAR MR. NANSEN: It is the earnest desire of the allied and associated Governments, and
of the peoples for whom they speak, to assuage the distress of the millions of men, women, and
children who are suffering in Russia. The associated powers have solemnly pledged their resources
to relieve the stricken regions of Europe. Their efforts, begun in Belgium and in Northern France
during the course of the war, now extend to exhausted peoples from Finland to the Dalmatian
coast. Ports long idle are busy again. Trainloads of food are moved into the interior and there are
distributed with an impartial hand. Industry is awakened, and life is resumed at the point where it
was broken off by war. These measures of relief will be continued until nations are once more able
to provide for their needs through the normal channels of commerce.

The associated peoples desire and deem it their duty similarly to assist in relieving the people
of Russia from the misery, famine, and disease which oppress them. In view of the responsibilities
which have already been undertaken by the associated Governments they welcome the suggestion
that the neutral States should take the initiative in the matter of Russian relief and, therefore, are
prepared to state in accordance with your request, the conditions under which they will approve and
assist a neutral commission for the provisioning of Russia.

The allied and associated Governments and all Governments now exercising political
authority within the territory of the former Russian Empire, including Finland, together with
Poland, Galicia, Roumania, Armenia, Azerbaidjan, and Afghanistan, shall agree that hostilities
against one another shall cease on all fronts within these territories on April 20 at noon; that fresh
hostilities shall not be begun during the period of this armistice, and that no troops or war material
of any kind whatever shall be transferred to or within these territories so long as the armistice shall
continue. The duration of the armistice shall be for two weeks unless extended by mutual consent.

The allied and associated Governments propose that such of these Governments as are
willing to accept the terms of this armistice, shall send not more than three representatives each,
together with necessary technical experts, to Christiania, where they shall meet on April 25 with
representatives of the allied and associated Governments in conference to discuss peace 'and the
provisioning of Russia, upon the basis of the following principles:

1. All signatory Governments shall remain, as against each other, in full control of the
territories which they occupy at the moment when the armistice becomes effective, subject to such
rectifications as may be agreed upon by the conference, or until the peoples inhabiting these
territories shall themselves voluntarily determine to change their government.

2. The right of free entry, sojourn, circulation, and full security shall be accorded by the
several signatories to the citizens of each other; provided, however, that such persons comply with
the laws of the country to which they seek admittance, and provided also-that they do not interfere
or attempt to interfere in any way with the domestic politics of that country.

3. The right to send official representatives enjoying full liberty and immunity shall be
accorded by the several signatories to one another.

4. A general amnesty shall be granted by the various signatories to all political or military opponents, offenders, and prisoners who are so treated because of their association or affiliation with another signatory, provided that they have not otherwise violated the laws of the land.

5. Nationals of one signatory residing or detained in the country of another shall be given all possible facilities for repatriation.

6. The allied and associated Governments will immediately withdraw their armed forces and further military support from the territory of the former Russian Empire, including Finland and the various Governments within that territory shall effect a simultaneous reduction of armed forces according to a scheme of demobilization and control to be agreed upon by the conference.

7. Any economic blockade imposed by one signatory as against another shall be lifted and trade relations shall be established, subject to a program of equitable distribution of supplies and utilization of transport facilities to be agreed upon by the conference in consultation with representatives of those neutral States which are prepared to assume the responsibility for the provisioning of Russia.

8. Provision shall be made by the conference for a mutual exchange of transit and port privileges among the several signatories.

9. The Governments which have been set up on the territory of the former Russian Empire and Finland shall recognize their responsibility for the financial obligations of the former Russian Empire to foreign States parties to this agreement and to the nationals of such States. Detailed arrangements for discharging these obligations shall be agreed upon by the conference, regard being had to the present financial situation of Russia.

10. The conference shall be competent to discuss and determine any other matter which bears upon the provisioning of Russia, the problem of establishing peace within the territory of the former Russian Empire, including Finland, and the reestablishment of international relations among the signatories.

Mr. BULLITT. I also prepared at the orders of Col. House————

Senator KNOX. What attitude did you take toward the Nansen proposal?

Mr. BULLITT. At first I opposed it. I was in favor of the original plan.

Senator KNOX. You were in favor of the original plan?

Mr. BULLITT. I was in favor of direct, straightforward action in the matter. However, I found that there was no use in kicking against the pricks, that I was unable to persuade the commission that my point of view was the correct one. Therefore at the request of Col. House I wrote out a reply to Dr. Nansen, in which I embodied a peace proposal so that it would have meant a peace conference via Nansen, which was what was desired.

Senator BRANDEGEE. Was that letter delivered to Nansen?

Mr. BULLITT. No. I gave this reply of mine to Col. House. Col. House read it and said he would approve it, but that before he gave it to the President and to Lloyd George as his solution of the way to deal with this Russian matter, he wished it considered by his international law experts, Mr. Auchincloss and Mr. Miller, and it was thereupon turned over that afternoon to Mr. Auchincloss and Mr. Miller. Does the Senator desire this document?

Senator KNOX. I do not regard it as material. It was not accepted?

Mr. BULLITT. It was not accepted. What happened in regard to this was that Mr. Auchincloss and Mr. Miller, to correct its legal language, produced a proposition which was entirely different, which left out all possibility of the matter coming to a peace conference, and was largely an offer to feed Russia provided Russia put all her railroads in the hands of the allied and associated Governments. I have that as well.

Senator BRANDEGEE. Do you object to having that put in the record, Senator Knox?

Senator KNOX. No.

Senator BRANDEGEE. I would like to have that put in.

(The document referred to is here printed in full, as follows:)

(AUCHINCLOSS-MILLER PROPOSAL)

Draft of proposed letter to be signed by President Wilson and the prime ministers of Great Britain, France, and Italy in reply to Mr. Nansen's letter:

DEAR SIR: The situation of misery and suffering in Russia which is described in your letter of April 3 is one which appeals to the sympathies of all peoples of the world. Regardless of political differences or shades of thought, the knowledge that thousands and perhaps millions of men, and above all of women and children lack the food and the necessities which make life endurable is one which is shocking to humanity.

The Governments and the peoples whom we represent, without thought of political, military or financial advantage, would be glad to cooperate in any proposal which would relieve the existing situation in Russia. It seems to us that such a commission as you propose, purely humanitarian in its purpose, would offer a practical means of carrying out the beneficent results which you have in view and could not either in its conception or its operation be considered as having in view any other aim than "the humanitarian purpose of saving life."

It is true that there are great difficulties to be overcome, political difficulties owing to the existing situation in Russia, and difficulties of supply and transport. But if the existing de facto governments of Russia are all willing as the Governments and peoples whom we represent to see succor and relief given to the stricken peoples of Russia, no political difficulties will remain as obstacles thereto.

There will remain, however, the difficulties of supply and transport which we have mentioned and also the problem of distribution in Russia itself. The problem of supply we can ourselves safely hope to solve in connection with the advice and cooperation of such a commission as you propose. The problem of transport of supplies to Russia we can hope to meet with the assistance of your own and other neutral Governments.

The difficulties of transport in Russia can in large degree only be overcome in Russia itself. So far as possible, we would endeavor to provide increased means of transportation; but we would consider it essential in any such scheme of relief that control of transportation in Russia, so far as was necessary in the distribution of relief supplies, should be placed wholly under such a commission as is described in your letter and should to the necessary extent be freed from any governmental or private control whatsoever.

The real human element in the situation, even supposing all these difficulties to be surmounted, is the problem of distribution, the problem of seeing that the food reaches the starving, the medicines the sick, the clothing the naked. Subject to the supervision of such a commission, this is a problem which should be solely under the control of the people of Russia themselves so far as it is humanly possible to put it under their control. It is not a question of class or of race or of politics but a question of human beings in need, and these human beings in each locality should be given, as under the regime of the Belgian relief commission, the fullest opportunity to advise the commission upon the methods and the personnel by which their community is to be relieved. Under no other circumstances could it be believed that the purpose of this relief was humanitarian and not political, and still more important, under no other conditions could it be certain that the hungry would be fed. That such a course would involve cessation of hostilities by Russian troops would of course mean a cessation of all hostilities on the Russian fronts. Indeed, relief to Russia which did not mean a return to a state of peace would be futile, and would be impossible to consider.

Under such conditions as we have outlined, we believe that your plan could be successfully carried into effect and we should be prepared to give it our full support.

Senator KNOX. What I am anxious to get at is to find out what became of your report.

Senator FALL. I should like to know whether Col. House approved Mr. Auchincloss's and Mr. Miller's report, or the report of the witness.

Mr. BULLITT. I should like to have this clear, and if I can read just this one page I shall be greatly obliged. On this proposition I wrote the following memorandum to Mr. Auchincloss [reading]:

APRIL 4, 1919.

Memorandum for Mr. Auchincloss:

DEAR GORDON: I have studied carefully the draft of the reply to Dr. Nansen which you have prepared. In spirit and substance your letter differs so radically from the reply which I consider essential that I find it difficult to make any constructive criticism. And I shall refrain from criticizing your rhetoric.

31

There are two proposals in your letter, however, which are obviously unfair and will not, I am certain, be accepted by the Soviet Government.

1. The life of Russia depends upon its railroads; and your demand for control of transportation by the commission can hardly be accepted by the Soviet Government which knows that plots for the destruction of railroad bridges were hatched in the American consulate in Moscow. You are asking the Soviet Government to put its head in the lion's mouth. It will not accept. You must moderate your phrases.

2. When you speak of the "cessation of hostilities by Russian troops," you fail to speak of hostilities by troops of the allied and associated Governments, a number of whom, you may recall, have invaded Russia. Furthermore, your phrase does not cover Finns, Esthonians, Letts, Poles, etc. In addition, you say absolutely nothing about the withdrawal of the troops of the allied and associated Governments from Russian territory. And, most important, you fail to say that troops and military supplies will cease to be sent into the territory of the former Russian Empire. You thereby go a long way toward proving Trotsky's thesis: That any armistice will simply be used by the Allies as a period in which to supply tanks, aeroplanes, gas shells, liquid fire, etc., to the various antisoviet governments. As it stands, your armistice proposal is absolutely unfair, and I am sure that it will not be accepted by the Soviet Government.

Very respectfully, yours,

WILLIAM C. BULLITT.

Senator NEW. Otherwise you had no fault to find with it?

Mr. BULLITT. Yes. The morning after Col. House had told me he wished to submit this proposition to his international law experts, I came as usual to his office about 9.40, and Mr. Auchincloss was on his way to the President with his proposal, the Auchincloss-Miller proposal, as Col. House's proposal. But I got that stopped. I went in to Col. House, and Col. House told Mr. Auchincloss not to take it up to the President, and asked me if I could doctor up the reply of Mr. Auchincloss and Mr. Miller to the Nansen letter so that it might possibly be acceptable to the Soviet Government. I thereupon rewrote the Auchincloss-Miller letter, but I was forced to stick very closely to the text. I was told that I could cut things out if I wished to, but to stick very closely to the text, which I did. I drew this redraft of their letter, under protest at the whole business. My redraft of their letter was finally the basis of the reply of the four to Nansen. I have both these documents here, my reply—and the four took that reply—and with the changes——

The CHAIRMAN. What four—the successors of the ten?

Mr. BULLITT. The successors of the 10, sir, took the reply——

The CHAIRMAN. Who were the four at that moment?

Mr. BULLITT. M. Orlando, Mr. Lloyd George, M. Clemenceau, and the President. This extremely mild proposition, which really had almost no chance of life, was, you will see, in no sense a reply to these proposals of the Soviet Government. This is my attempt to doctor up the Auchincloss-Miller proposition. In spite of every effort I could make to obtain definite action on it, the reply was made to me that this reply to the Nansen proposal would be a sufficient reply to that proposal of the Soviet Government. [Reading:]

DEAR SIR: The misery and suffering in Russia described in your letter of April 3 appeals to the sympathies of all peoples. It is shocking to humanity that millions of men, women, and children lack the food and the necessities, which make life endurable.

The Governments and peoples whom we represent would be glad to cooperate, without thought of political, military, or financial advantage, in any proposal which would relieve this situation in Russia. It seems to us that such a commission as you propose would offer a practical means of achieving the beneficent results you have in view, and could not, either in its conception or its operation, be considered as having any other aim than the "humanitarian purpose of saving life."

There are great difficulties to be overcome, political difficulties, owing to the existing situation in Russia, and difficulties of supply and transport. But if the existing local governments of Russia are as willing as the Governments and the peoples whom we represent to see succor and relief given to the stricken peoples of Russia, no political obstacle will remain. There will remain, however, the difficulties of supply and transport, which we have mentioned, and also the problem of distribution in Russia itself. The problem of supply we can ourselves hope to solve, in connection with the

32

advice and cooperation of such a commission as you propose. The problem of transport of supplies to Russia we can hope to meet with the assistance of your own and other neutral Governments. The problem of transport in Russia and of distribution can be solved only by the people of Russia themselves, with the assistance, advice, and supervision of your commission.

Subject to such supervision, the problem of distribution should be solely under the control of the people of Russia themselves. The people in each locality should be given, as under the regime of the Belgian Relief Commission, the fullest opportunity to advise your commission upon the methods and the personnel by which their community is to be relieved. In no other circumstances could it be believed that the purpose of this relief was humanitarian, and not political, under no other conditions could it be certain that the hungry would be fed.

That such a course would involve cessation of all hostilities within the territory of the former Russian Empire is obvious. And the cessation of hostilities would, necessarily, involve a complete suspension of the transfer of troops and military material of all sorts to and within these territories. Indeed, relief to Russia which did not mean a return to a state of peace would be futile, and would be impossible to consider.

Under such conditions as we have outlined we believe that your plan could be successfully carried into effect, and we should be prepared to give it our full support.

REPLY OF PRESIDENT WILSON, PREMIERS CLEMENCEAU, LLOYD GEORGE, AND ORLANDO, TO DR. NANSEN, APRIL 17, 1919

DEAR SIR: The misery and suffering in Russia described in your letter of April 3 appeals to the sympathies of all peoples. It is shocking to humanity that millions of men, women, and children lack the food and the necessities which make life endurable.

The Governments and peoples whom we represent would be glad to cooperate, without thought of political, military, or financial advantage, in any proposal which would relieve this situation in Russia. It seems to us that such a commission as you propose would offer a practical means of achieving the beneficent results you have in view, and could not, either in its conception or its operation, be considered as having any other aim than the "humanitarian purpose of saving life."

There are great difficulties to be overcome, political difficulties, owing to the existing situation in Russia, and difficulties of supply and transport. But if the existing local governments of Russia are as willing as the Governments and people whom we represent to see succor and relief given to the stricken peoples of Russia, no political obstacle will remain.

There will remain, however, the difficulties of supply, finance, and transport which we have mentioned? and also the problem of distribution in Russia itself. The problem of supply we can ourselves hope to solve, in connection with the advice and cooperation of such a commission as you propose. The problem of finance would seem to us to fall upon the Russian authorities. The problem of transport of supplies to Russia we can hope to meet with the assistance of your own and other neutral governments whose interests should be as great as our own and whose losses have been far less. The problems of transport in Russia and of distribution can be solved only by the people of Russia themselves, with the assistance, advice, and supervision of your commission.

Subject to your supervision, the problem of distribution should be solely under the control of the people of Russia themselves. The people in each locality should be given, as under the regime of the Belgian Relief Commission, the fullest opportunity to advise your commission upon the methods and the personnel by which their community is to be relieved. In no other circumstances could it be believed that the purpose of this relief was humanitarian, and not political; under no other condition could it be certain that the hungry would be fed.

That such a course would involve cessation of all hostilities within definitive lines in the territory of Russia is obvious. And the cessation of hostilities would, necessarily, involve a complete suspension of the transfer of troops and military material of all sorts to and within Russian territory. Indeed, relief to Russia which did not mean a return to a state of peace would be futile and would be impossible to consider.

Under such conditions as we have outlined, we believe that your plan could be successfully carried into effect, and we should be prepared to give it our full support.

V.E. ORLANDO. D. LLOYD GEORGE. WOODROW WILSON. G. CLEMENCEAU.

Senator KNOX. I want the reply of Auchincloss to Nansen to go into the record.

The CHAIRMAN. Let all that correspondence be printed in the record.

Senator KNOX. Dr. Nansen's proposition, and then the reply,

(The letters referred to are inserted above.)

Mr. BULLITT. The Nansen letter was written in Mr. Hoover's office. Nansen made the proposition. I wrote the original of a reply to Dr. Nansen, which I believe would have led to peace. Col. House indicated his approval of it, but wished to have it considered from the international legal standpoint, which was then done by Mr. Auchincloss and Mr. Miller, who proposed a reply that had no resemblance to my proposal. I then objected to that as it was on its way to the President. It was not sent to the President, and I was ordered to try to doctor it up. I attempted to doctor it up and produced a doctored version which was finally made the basis of the reply, with the change of two or three words which made it even worse and even more indefinite, so that the Soviet Government could not possibly conceive it as a genuine peace proposition. It left the whole thing in the air.

Senator KNOX. We would like to have you see that these documents to which you have just now referred are inserted in the record in the sequence in which you have named them.

Mr. BULLITT. Yes, I shall be at the service of the committee in that regard.

Senator HARDING. Lest I missed something while I was out of the room I am exceedingly curious to know why the Soviet proposal was not given favorable consideration.

Senator KNOX. Mr. Bullitt has stated that.

KOLCHAK'S ADVANCE CAUSES REJECTION OF PEACE PROPOSAL

Mr. BULLITT. The principal reason was entirely different. The fact was that just at this moment, when this proposal was under consideration, Kolchak made a 100-mile advance. There was a revolt of peasants in a district of Russia which entirely cut off supplies from the Bolshevik army operating against Kolchak. Kolchak made a 100-mile advance, and immediately the entire press of Paris was roaring and screaming on the subject, announcing that Kolchak would be in Moscow within two weeks; and therefore everyone in Paris, including, I regret to say members of the American commission, began to grow very lukewarm about peace in Russia, because they thought Kolchak would arrive in Moscow and wipe out the Soviet Government.

Senator KNOX. And the proposal which you brought back from Russia, that is the Soviet proposal, was abandoned and dropped, after this last document to which you have just referred.

Mr. BULLITT. Yes; it was. May I say this, that April 10 was the final date when their proposition was open. I had attempted every day and almost every night to obtain a reply to it. I finally requested the commission to send the following telegram to Tchitcherin.

I proposed to send this telegram to the American consul at Helsingfors [reading]:

APRIL 10, 1919.

AMERICAN CONSUL, Helsingfors:

Please send Kock or other reliable person immediately to
Petrograd to Schklovsky, minister of foreign affairs, with
following message for Tchitcherin:

"Action leading to food relief via neutrals likely within
week.—Bullitt."

AMMISSION.

The commission considered that matter, and this is the official minute of their meeting [reading]:

AMERICAN MISSION TO NEGOTIATE PEACE,

[No. 211.] April 10, 1919.

To: The Commissioners, for action.

Subject: Telegram to Tchitcherin.

Statement.—Action by the council of four on the reply to Mr. Nansen was prevented yesterday by French objection to a minor clause in the President's letter. It is hoped that agreement in this matter may be reached to-day or to-morrow, but it is quite possible that agreement may not be reached for several days.

To-day, April 10, the pledge of the Soviet Government to accept a proposal of the sort outlined in its statement of March 14 expires. No indication has been given the Soviet Government that its statement was ever placed before the conference of Paris or that any change of policy in regard to Russia is contemplated. In view of the importance which the Soviet Government placed

34

upon its statement, I fear that this silence and the passing of April 10 will be interpreted as a definite rejection of the peace effort of the Soviet Government and that the Soviet Government will at once issue belligerent political statements and orders for attacks on all fronts, including Bessarabia and Archangel. It is certain that if the soviet troops should enter Bessarabia or should overcome the allied forces at Archangel, the difficulty of putting through the policy which is likely to be adopted within the next few days would be greatly increased. I feel that if the appended telegram should be sent at once to Tchitcherin, no large offensive movements by the soviet armies would be undertaken for another week, and no provocative political statements would be issued.

I therefore respectfully suggest that the appended telegram should be sent at once.
Respectfully submitted.
WILLIAM C. BULLITT.
APRIL 10, 1919.

At the meeting of the commissioners this morning the above memorandum was read in which Mr. Bullitt requested that a telegram be sent to the American consul at Helsingfors, instructing the latter to send a message through reliable sources to Tchitcherin respecting Mr. Lansing's contemplated scheme for relief in Russia. After some discussion the commissioners redrafted the telegram in question to read as follows:

"Please send Kock or other reliable person immediately to Petrograd to Schklovsky, minister of foreign affairs, with following message for Tchitcherin, sent on my personal responsibility: 'Individuals of neutral States are considering organization for feeding Russia. Will perhaps decide something definite within a week.'—Bullitt."

CHRISTIAN A. HERTER,
Assistant to Mr. White.

I believe that telegram was dispatched. I do not know.

Senator KNOX. Mr. Bullitt, I want to ask you a question. You have told us that you went to Russia with instructions from the Secretary of State, Mr. Lansing, with a definition of the American policy by Mr. House, with the approval of Lloyd George, who approved of your mission, of the purposes for which you were being sent. Now, tell us whether or not to your knowledge your report and the proposal of the Soviet Government was ever formally taken up by the peace conference and acted on?

Mr. BULLITT. It was never formally laid before the peace conference, which I believe met only six times during the course of the entire proceedings of what is called the peace conference.

LLOYD GEORGE DECEIVES PARLIAMENT

Senator KNOX. Did not Mr. Lloyd George in a speech to Parliament assert that he had never received the proposal with which you returned from Russia? Have you a copy of his speech?

Mr. BULLITT. About a week after I had handed to Mr. Lloyd George the official proposal, with my own hands, in the presence of three other persons, he made a speech before the British Parliament, and gave the British people to understand that he knew nothing whatever about any such proposition. It was a most egregious case of misleading the public, perhaps the boldest that I have ever known in my life. On the occasion of that statement of Mr. Lloyd George, I wrote the President. I clipped his statement from a newspaper and sent it to the President, and I asked the President to inform me whether the statement of Mr. Lloyd George was true or untrue. He was unable to answer, inasmuch as he would have had to reply on paper that Mr. Lloyd George had made an untrue statement. So flagrant was this that various members of the British mission called on me at the Crillon, a day or so later, and apologized for the Prime Minister's action in the case.

Senator KNOX. Have you a copy of Lloyd George's remarks in the Parliament?

Mr. BULLITT. I have a copy.
Senator KNOX. Suppose you read it?
Mr. BULLITT. It is as follows:

Mr. CLYNES. Before the right honorable gentleman comes to the next subject, can he make any statement on the approaches or representations alleged to have been made to his Government by persons acting on behalf of such government as there is in Central Russia?

Mr. LLOYD GEORGE. We have had no approaches at all except what have appeared in the papers.

Mr. CLYNES. I ask the question because it has been repeatedly alleged.

Mr. LLOYD GEORGE. We have had no approaches at all. Constantly there are men coming and going to Russia of all nationalities, and they always come back with their tales of Russia. But we have made no approach of any sort.

I have only heard reports of others having proposals which they assume have come from authentic quarters, but these have never been put before the peace conference by any member, and therefore we have not considered them.

I think I know what my right honorable friend refers to. There was some suggestion that a young American had come back from Russia with a communication. It is not for me to judge the value of this communication, but if the President of the United States had attached any value to it he would have brought it before the conference, and he certainly did not.

It was explained to me by the members of the British delegation who called on me, that the reason for this deception was that although when Lloyd George got back to London he intended to make a statement very favorable to peace with Russia, he found that Lord Northcliffe, acting through Mr. Wickham Steed, the editor of The Times, and Mr. Winston Churchill, British secretary for war, had rigged the conservative majority of the House of Commons against him, and that they were ready to slay him then and there if he attempted to speak what was his own opinion at the moment on Russian policies.

MR. BULLITT RESIGNS

Senator KNOX. Mr. Bullitt, you resigned your relations with the State Department and the public service, did you not?

Mr. BULLITT. I did, sir.

Senator KNOX. When?

Mr. BULLITT. I resigned on May 17.

Senator KNOX. For what reason?

Mr. BULLITT. Well, I can explain that perhaps more briefly than in any other way by reading my letter of resignation to the President, which is brief.

Senator KNOX. Very well, we would like to hear it.

The CHAIRMAN. Before that letter is read, you did not see the President and had no knowledge of his attitude in regard to your report?

Mr. BULLITT. None whatever, except as it was reported to me by Col. House. Col. House, as I said before, reported to me that he thought in the first place that the President favored the peace proposal; in the second place, that the President could not turn his mind to it, because he was too occupied with Germany, and finally—well, really, I have no idea what was in the President's mind.

Senator KNOX. There never was another effort to secure an audience with the President for you after those first two that you say Col. House made?

Mr. BULLITT. No; not at all. Meetings with the President were always arranged through Col. House.

In my letter of resignation to the President, which was dated May 17, 1919, I said:

MAY 17, 1919.

MY DEAR MR. PRESIDENT: I have submitted to-day to the Secretary of State my resignation as an assistant in the Department of State, attaché to the American commission to negotiate peace. I was one of the millions who trusted confidently and implicitly in your leadership and believed that you would take nothing less than "a permanent peace" based upon "unselfish and unbiased justice." But our Government has consented now to deliver the suffering peoples of the world to new oppressions, subjections, and dismemberments—a new century of war. And I can convince myself no longer that effective labor for "a new world order" is possible as a servant of this Government.

Russia, "the acid test of good will," for me as for you, has not even been understood. Unjust decisions of the conference in regard to Shantung, the Tyrol, Thrace, Hungary, East Prussia, Danzig, the Saar Valley, and the abandonment of the principle of the freedom of the seas make new international conflicts certain. It is my conviction that the present league of nations will be powerless-to prevent these wars, and that the United States will be involved in them by the obligations undertaken in the covenant of the league and in the special understanding with France.

Therefore the duty of the Government of the United States to its own people and to mankind is to refuse to sign or ratify this unjust treaty, to refuse to guarantee its settlements by entering the league of nations, to refuse to entangle the United States further by the understanding with France.

That you personally opposed most of the unjust settlements, and that you accepted them only under great pressure, is well known. Nevertheless, it is my conviction that if you had made your fight in the open, instead of behind closed doors, you would have carried with you the public opinion of the world, which was yours; you would have been able to resist the pressure and might have established the "new international order based upon broad and universal principles of right and justice" of which you used to speak. I am sorry that you did not fight our fight to the finish and that you had so little faith in the millions of men, like myself, in every nation who had faith in you.

Very sincerely, yours,

WILLIAM C. BULLITT.

To the honorable WOODROW WILSON,

President of the United States.

Senator KNOX. Did you ever get a reply to that letter?

Mr. BULLITT. I did not, sir. The only intimation I had in regard to it was that Mr. Close, secretary of the President, with whom I was lunching, said to me that the President had read my letter and had said that he would not reply. In connection with that I wrote Col. House a letter at the same time as follows:

MAY 17, 1919.

MY DEAR COL. HOUSE: Since you kindly lent me the text of the proposed treaty of peace, I have tried to convince myself that some good might come of it and that I ought to remain in the service of the Department of State to labor for its establishment.

It is with sincere regret that I have come to the conviction that no good ever will issue from a thing so evil and that those who care about a permanent peace should oppose the signature and ratification of it, and of the special understanding with France.

I have therefore submitted my resignation to the Secretary of State and have written the appended note to the President. I hope you will bring it to his attention; not because he will care what I may think, but because I have expressed the thoughts which are in the minds of many young and old men in the commission—thoughts which the President will have to reckon with when the world begins to reap the crop of wars the seeds of which have here been sown.

I feel sure that you will agree that I am right in acting on my conviction and I hope that this action will in no way affect the relationship between us which has always been so delightful and stimulating to me.

With my sincerest personal regards, I am, Very respectfully, yours,

WILLIAM C. BULLITT.

To the honorable EDWARD M. HOUSE,

Hotel Crillon, Paris.

Senator KNOX. Did you get a reply to that?

Mr. BULLITT. Col. House sent for me, and after that we had a conversation. That was the only reply that I had. I had a conversation with Col. House on the whole matter, and we thrashed it all out.

Senator KNOX. Was anything said during this conversation which you feel willing or disposed to tell us, which will be important?

Mr. BULLITT. I made a record of the conversation. Inasmuch as the conversations which I had with various members of the commission on the occasion of my resignation touched on a number of important issues, I kept a record of those conversations, that is, those I had at the time when I resigned. They are the only conversations of which I made records, and I made them simply because we did deal more or less with the entire question of the peace treaty. On the other hand, they are personal conversations, and I hesitate to repeat them, unless the committee considers it particularly important.

Senator KNOX. I would not press you on the personal conversations which you had with Col. House after you resigned. I leave the matter to your own judgment. I wondered whether there might have been something which transpired which you would care to tell us; but I withdraw that suggestion. I should like to ask you this one question: I suppose your letter of resignation to Mr. Lansing was merely formal?

Mr. BULLITT. My letter of resignation to Mr. Lansing was a formal letter.

Senator KNOX. You certainly got a reply to that.

Mr. BULLITT. I did, sir. I wrote a formal letter and I got a formal reply, and the Secretary sent for me the same afternoon and explained that he only sent me a formal reply because it was necessary, because of the form in which I had put my resignation, and particularly because I had appended to my note my letter to the President. We then discussed various other matters in connection with the treaty.

The CHAIRMAN. Are you through?

Senator KNOX. Yes.

The CHAIRMAN. Mr. Bullitt, you put into the record or read here, I think, some extracts from the minutes of the Council of Ten?

Mr. BULLITT. Yes, sir.

The CHAIRMAN. Were you present at any of these meetings?

Mr. BULLITT. I was not, sir.

The CHAIRMAN. The Council of Ten was the first body that was dealing with the treaty generally, the important body? It was not a special commission?

Mr. BULLITT. No, sir. It was the main body of the conference.

The CHAIRMAN. Yes; it was the main body, and was the one that subsequently became the Council of Five, and then the Council of Four, and I think at one time a Council of Three?

Mr. BULLITT. Yes, sir.

The CHAIRMAN. Well, now, there were records of these meetings, were there not?

Mr. BULLITT. Yes, sir.

The CHAIRMAN. Do you know what disposition was made of those records?

Mr. BULLITT. Mr. Chairman, there were a number of copies for each delegation, and I presume that there must be a number of copies in this country at the present time; perhaps not.

The CHAIRMAN. You say each delegate had a copy?

Mr. BULLITT. Each plenipotentiary had a copy, and the Secretary of the American Commission had a copy, I believe, and the assistant secretaries had copies; certainly one of the assistant secretaries, Mr. Leland Harrison; and Mr. Grew had a copy.

The CHAIRMAN. Did Mr. Lansing have copies while he served on the Council of Ten?

Mr. BULLITT. Yes, sir; well, I am quite sure that he did. I am sure that I have seen copies on the desk of the Secretary.

The CHAIRMAN. Well, they were furnished regularly to every member of the conference?

Mr. BULLITT. Yes.

The CHAIRMAN. We have found some difficulty in getting them; that is the reason I asked.

Senator KNOX. I am informed—perhaps Mr. Bullitt can tell us—that there is a complete set of minutes in the hands of some individual in this country. Do you know anything about that— perhaps Auchincloss & Miller?

Mr. BULLITT. I could not be certain in regard to the matter, but I should certainly be under the impression that Mr. Auchincloss and Mr. Miller have copies of the minutes; perhaps not. Perhaps Mr. Auchincloss has left his with Col. House. He would have Col. House's copies. Perhaps they are in this country, perhaps not. But Mr. Auchincloss and Mr. Miller perhaps have those minutes in their files.

The CHAIRMAN. Undoubtedly there are a number, at least, of those records in existence.

Mr. BULLITT. Certainly, sir.

The CHAIRMAN. That must be the case.

Mr. BULLITT. Certainly, sir. Also records of the meetings of the American Commission.

Senator BRANDEGEE. Do you know whether or not they are in the State Department—any of these minutes or records in our State Department?

38

Mr. BULLITT. I should presume that in the normal course of events they would be certainly among Mr. Lansing's papers, which were very carefully kept. He had an excellent secretariat.

The CHAIRMAN. Did any member of our delegation, any member of the council of 10, express to you any opinions about the general character of this treaty?

Mr. BULLITT. Well, Mr. Lansing, Col. House, Gen. Bliss, and Mr. White had all expressed to me very vigorously their opinions on the subject.

The CHAIRMAN. Were they enthusiastically in favor of it?

Mr. BULLITT. I regret to say, not.

As I say, the only documents of the sort that I have are the memoranda of the discussions that I had after I resigned, when we thrashed over the whole ground.

The CHAIRMAN. Those memoranda of consultations that you had after you resigned you prefer not to publish? I am not asking you to do so.

Mr. BULLITT. I think it would be out of the way.

The CHAIRMAN. I quite understand your position. I only wanted to know—I thought it might be proper for you to say whether or not their opinions which you heard them express were favorable to the series of arrangements, I would call them, that were made for the consideration of this treaty.

Mr. BULLITT. It is no secret that Mr. Lansing, Gen. Bliss, and Mr. Henry White objected very vigorously to the numerous provisions of the treaty.

The CHAIRMAN. It is known that they objected to Shantung. That, I think, is public information. I do not know that it is public information that they objected to anything else.

Mr. BULLITT. I do not think that Secretary Lansing is at all enthusiastic about the league of nations as it stands at present. I have a note of a conversation with him on the subject, which, if I may, I will just read, without going into the rest of that conversation, because it bears directly on the issue involved.

This was a conversation with the Secretary of State at 2.30 on May 19. The Secretary sent for me. It was a long conversation, and Mr. Lansing in the course of it said:

Mr. Lansing then said that he personally would have strengthened greatly the judicial clauses of the league of nations covenant, making arbitration compulsory. He also said that he was absolutely opposed to the United States taking a mandate in either Armenia or Constantinople; that he thought that Constantinople should be placed under a local government, the chief members of which were appointed by an international committee.

This is a matter, it seems to me, of some importance in regard to the whole discussion, and therefore I feel at liberty to read it, as it is not a personal matter.

The CHAIRMAN. This is a note of the conversation made at the time?

Mr. BULLITT. This is a note which I immediately dictated after the conversation. [Reading:]

Mr. Lansing then said that he, too, considered many parts of the treaty thoroughly bad, particularly those dealing with Shantung and the league of nations. He said: "I consider that the league of nations at present is entirely useless. The great powers have simply gone ahead and arranged the world to suit themselves. England and France in particular have gotten out of the treaty everything that they wanted, and the league of nations can do nothing to alter any of the unjust clauses of the treaty except by unanimous consent of the members of the league, and the great powers will never give their consent to changes in the interests of weaker peoples."

We then talked about the possibility of ratification by the Senate. Mr. Lansing said: "I believe that if the Senate could only understand what this treaty means, and if the American people could really understand, it would unquestionably be defeated, but I wonder if they will ever understand what it lets them in for." He expressed the opinion that Mr. Knox would probably really understand the treaty— [Laughter.] May I reread it?

He expressed the opinion that Mr. Knox would probably really understand the treaty, and that Mr. Lodge would; but that Mr. Lodge's position would become purely political, and therefore ineffective.

[Laughter.]

The CHAIRMAN. I do not mind.

Mr. BULLITT (reading):

He thought, however, that Mr. Knox might instruct America in the real meaning of it.

[Laughter.]

The CHAIRMAN. He has made some very valuable efforts in the direction.

Mr. BULLITT. I beg to be excused from reading any more of these conversations.

Senator BRANDEGEE. We get the drift.

[Laughter.]

I want to ask one or two questions.

The CHAIRMAN. Go ahead.

Senator BRANDEGEE. Did you read any of these minutes of the meetings of the American commission?

Mr. BULLITT. Of the American commission itself?

Senator BRANDEGEE. Yes.

Mr. BULLITT. No, sir. I have on one or two occasions glanced at them but I never have read them carefully.

Senator BRANDEGEE. They were accessible to you at the time, were they?

Mr. BULLITT. They were, sir.

Senator BRANDEGEE. You stated, if I recall your testimony correctly, that when the proposition was made that the legislative bodies of the contracting parties should have representation in the assembly, the President objected to that?

Mr. BULLITT. The President—if I may explain again—approved in principle, but said that he did not see how the thing could be worked out, and he felt that the assembly of delegates, or whatever it is called in the present draft, gave sufficient representation to the peoples of the various countries.

Senator BRANDEGEE. Do you know what his objection was to the legislative bodies of the contracting parties having representation on the assembly?

Mr. BULLITT. The President believed, I think—in fact, it was so stated to me by Col. House, who discussed the matter with me—that it would make too unwieldy a central organ for the league.

Senator BRANDEGEE. Do you understand why it would be any more unwieldy if Congress should appoint the delegates than if the President should?

Mr. BULLITT. It would necessitate a larger central body if representation was to be given to the important political parties of the various countries. It would have necessitated a body of, say, 10 representatives from the United States—5 from the Republican party and 5 from the; Democratic Party, in the assembly of the league, which would become a large body.

Senator BRANDEGEE. The idea was that the political parties of the country should be represented?

Mr. BULLITT. Yes, the political viewpoints should be represented so that you would get some connection between the central assembly of the league and the true opinion of the countries.

Senator BRANDEGEE. When you went across to Paris on the *George Washington* with the President do you know whether he had with him at that time any draft for a league of nations or any memorandum that he showed to you of discussed with you?

Mr. BULLITT. The President outlined to several of us one evening, or rather one afternoon, the conception he had at the time of the league of nations. I did not see any formal draft that he had, but the President made a statement before the council of 10, in one of these minutes from which I have been reading, stating that he had first—and in fact I think I know it from other sources—that he had first received the Phillimore report, that then it had been rewritten by Col. House and that he had rewritten Col. House's report, and after he had discussed his rewriting with Robert Cecil and Gen. Smuts, he had rewritten it again.

Senator BRANDEGEE. You stated substantially that the only part of the league draft which was laid before the Peace Conference which the President had his way about, was Article 10. Did you make some such statement as that?

Mr. BULLITT. Yes, sir.

Senator BRANDEGEE. The President stated to us that that was practically what he had submitted to the Niagara conference here when the ABC powers from South America were discussing the Mexican question. He had then considered it as an article for American use on this continent.

40

Do you know what the attitude of Gen Smuts was as to article 10 as proposed by the President?

Mr. BULLITT. I do not, sir. Again, full minutes of the discussions and conclusions reached of all these meetings of the committee on the league of nations were kept.

Senator BRANDEGEE. Did you read the various other plans that were proposed or suggested over there for a league of nations?

Mr. BULLITT. I have read some of them, sir.

Senator BRANDEGEE. Did the others have anything similar to what is now article 10 in the treaty pending in the Senate?

Mr. BULLITT. I really can not say. I am sorry, but I have forgotten. I should not care to testify on that.

Senator BRANDEGEE. Do you know from what you heard while you were there in your official capacity whether the other nations were anxious to have article 10 in the covenant for the league?

Mr. BULLITT. The French were not only anxious for it, but I believe were anxious greatly to strengthen it. They desired immediately a league army to be established, and I believe also to be stationed in Alsace-Lorraine and along the Rhine, in addition to article 10. I can not say for certain about the others.

The CHAIRMAN. Mr. Bullitt, we had before us at one of our hearings a representative of the Egyptian people. Do you know anything about that, when it was done, or any discussions about it? I mean the clauses that appear in regard to the British protectorate.

Mr. BULLITT. You mean our agreement to recognize the British protectorate in Egypt?

The CHAIRMAN. It was recognized by this treaty in those clauses.

Mr. BULLITT. Yes; but we gave a sort of assent before the treaty formally came out, did we not? I recall the morning it was done. It was handled by Sir William Wiseman, who was the confidential representative that Lloyd George and Balfour had constantly with Col. House and the President. He was a sort of extra confidential foreign office. It was all done, if I recall his statement correctly, in the course of one morning. The President was informed that the Egyptian nationalists were using his 14 points as meaning that the President thought that Egypt should have the right to control her own destinies, and therefore have independence, and that they were using this to foment revolution; that since the President had provoked this trouble by the 14 points, they thought that he should allay it by the statement that we would recognize the British protectorate, and as I remember Sir William Wiseman's statement to me that morning, he said that he had only brought up the matter that morning and that he had got our recognition of the British protectorate before luncheon.

The CHAIRMAN. The President made some public statement?

Mr. BULLITT. I am not certain in regard to the further developments of it. I recall that incident, that it was arranged through Sir William Wiseman, and that it took only a few minutes.

Senator KNOX. That was a good deal of time to devote to a little country like Egypt.

Mr. BULLITT. I do not know. You should know, sir, you have been Secretary of State.

Senator KNOX. We never chewed them up that fast.

Senator NEW. Mr. Bullitt, what, if anything, was said with reference to the Irish question, with which you are familiar?

Mr. BULLITT. At the conference? I do not believe the Irish question was ever brought up before the conference or discussed. There was considerable said on the side, attempts to let down the Walsh mission easily without antagonizing the Irish vote in this country. [Laughter.] I think that is the only consideration that Ireland received.

Senator NEW. There was a cheerful willingness to do that, was there not?

Mr. BULLITT. I think so.

The CHAIRMAN. Is there anything further that anybody desires to ask Mr. Bullitt? We are very much obliged to you indeed, Mr. Bullitt.

Mr. BULLITT. Mr. Chairman, if I may just say—I do not know whether it is a matter of first interest to the Senators or not—but on this trip with me to Russia there was Capt. Pettit, and at the

41

same time the journalist, Lincoln Steffens, and I have documents which they prepared and which might be of interest to the committee.

The CHAIRMAN. If you will hand those to the stenographer, we will print them with your testimony.

Senator KNOX. What are your plans, Mr. Bullitt? What are you going to do in this country now?

Mr. BULLITT. I expect to return to Maine and fish for trout, where I was when I was summoned by the committee.

Senator BRANDEGEE. Did Mr. Steffens go to Russia with you?

Mr. BULLITT. He did.

The CHAIRMAN. He held no official position?

Mr. BULLITT. No.

Senator BRANDEGEE. Who advised him to go?

Mr. BULLITT. I did.

Senator BRANDEGEE. Is he in the country now?

Mr. BULLITT. I do not believe so. I believe he is still in Europe.

REPORT OF LINCOLN STEFFENS

(By order of the committee the report of Lincoln Steffens referred to is here printed in full in the record, as follows:)

REPORT OF LINCOLN STEFFENS

APRIL 2, 1919.

Politically, Russia has reached a state of equilibrium; internally; for the present at least.

I think the revolution there is ended; that it has run its course. There will be changes. There may be advances; there will surely be reactions, but these will be regular, I think; political and economic, but parliamentary, A new center of gravity seems to have been found.

Certainly, the destructive phase of the revolution in Russia is over. Constructive work has begun.

We saw this everywhere. And we saw order, and though we inquired for them, we heard of no disorders. Prohibition is universal and absolute. Robberies have been reduced in Petrograd below normal of large cities. Warned against danger before we went in, we felt safe. Prostitution has disappeared with its clientele, who have been driven out by the "no-work-no-food law," enforced by the general want and the labor-card system. Loafing on the job by workers and sabotage by upper-class directors, managers, experts and clerks have been overcome. Russia has settled down to work.

The soviet form of government, which sprang up so spontaneously all over Russia, is established.

This is not a paper thing; not an invention. Never planned, it has not yet been written into the forms of law. It is not even uniform. It is full of faults and difficulties; clumsy, and in its final development it is not democratic. The present Russian Government is the most autocratic government I have ever seen. Lenin, head of the Soviet Government, is farther removed from the people than the Tsar was, or than any actual ruler in Europe is.

The people in a shop or an industry are a soviet. These little informal Soviets elect a local soviet; which elects delegates to the city or country (community) soviet; which elects delegates to the government (State) soviet. The government Soviets together elect delegates to the All-Russian Soviet, which elects commissionaires (who correspond to our Cabinet, or to a European minority). And these commissionaires finally elect Lenin. He is thus five or six removes from the people. To form an idea of his stability, independence, and power, think of the process that would have to be gone through with by the people to remove him and elect a successor. A majority of all the Soviets in all Russia would have to be changed in personnel or opinion, recalled, or brought somehow to recognize and represent the altered will of the people.

No student of government likes the soviet as it has developed. Lenin himself doesn't. He calls it a dictatorship, and he opposed it at first. When I was in Russia in the days of Milyoukov and Kerensky, Lenin and the Bolsheviks were demanding the general election of the constituent assembly. But the Soviets existed then; they had the power, and I saw foreign ambassadors blunder, and the world saw Milyoukov and Kerensky fall, partly because they would not, or could not, comprehend the nature of the soviet; as Lenin did finally, when, against his theory, he joined in and expressed the popular repudiation of the constituent assembly and went over to work with the soviet, the actual power in Russia. The constituent assembly, elected by the people, represented the upper class and the old system. The soviet was the lower class.

The soviet, at bottom, is a natural gathering of the working people, of peasants, in their working and accustomed groupings, instead of, as with us, by artificial geographical sections.

Labor unions and soldiers' messes made up the Soviets in the cities; poorer peasants and soldiers at the village inn were the first Soviets in the country; and in the beginning, two years ago, these lower class delegates used to explain to me that the "rich peasants" and the "rich people" had their own meetings and meeting places. The popular intention then was not to exclude the upper classes from the government, but only from the Soviets, which were not yet the same. But the Soviets, once in existence, absorbed in their own class tasks and their own problems, which the upper class had either not understood or solved, ignored—no; they simply forgot the council of empire and the Duma. And so they discovered (or, to be more exact, their leaders discovered) that they had actually all the power. All that Lenin and the other Socialist leaders had to do to carry through their class-struggle theory was to recognize this fact of power and teach the Soviets to continue to ignore the assemblies and the institutions of the upper classes, which, with their "governments," ministries, and local assemblies, fell, powerless from neglect.

The Soviet Government sprouted and grew out of the habits, the psychology, and the condition of the Russian people. It fitted them. They understand it. They find they can work it and they like it. Every effort to put something else in its place (including Lenin's) has failed. It will have to be modified, I think, but not in essentials, and it can not be utterly set aside. The Tsar himself, if he should come back, would have to keep the Russian Soviet, and somehow rule over and through it.

The Communist Party (dubbed "Bolshevik") is in power now in the Soviet Government.

I think it will stay there a long time. What I have shown of the machinery of change is one guaranty of communist dominance. There are others. All opposition to the communist government has practically ceased inside of Russia.

There are three organized opposition parties: Mencheviks, Social Revolutionary Right, and Social Revolutionary Left. The anarchists are not organized. The Social Revolutionary Left is a small group of very anarchistic leaders, who have hardly any following. The Mencheviks and the Social Revolutionaries Right are said to be strong, but there is no way of measuring their strength, for a very significant reason.

These parties have stopped fighting. They are critical, but they are not revolutionary. They also think the revolution is over. They proposed, and they still propose eventually, to challenge and oust the Communist Party by parliamentary and political methods, not by force. But when intervention came upon distracted Russia, and the people realized they were fighting many enemies on many fronts, the two strong opposing parties expressed their own and the public will to stand by the party in power until the menace of foreign invasion was beaten off. These parties announced this in formal statements, uttered by their regular conventions; you have confirmation of it in the memoranda written for you by Martov and Volsky, and you will remember how one of them put it to us personally:

"There is a fight to be made against the Bolsheviks, but so long as you foreigners are making it, we Russians won't. When you quit and leave us alone, we will take up our burden again, and we shall deal with the Bolsheviks. And we will finish them. But we will do it with our people, by political methods, in the Soviets, and not by force, not by war or by revolution, and not with any outside foreign help."

This is the nationalistic spirit, which we call patriotism, and understand perfectly; it is much stronger in the new than it was in the old, the Tsar's, Russia. But there is another force back of this remarkable statement of a remarkable state of mind.

All Russia has turned to the labor of reconstruction; sees the idea in the plans proposed for the future; and is interested—imaginatively.

Destruction was fun for a while and a satisfaction to a suppressed, betrayed, to an almost destroyed people. Violence was not in their character, however. The Russian people, sober, are said to be a gentle people. One of their poets speaks of them as "that gentle beast, the Russian people," and I noticed and described in my reports of the first revolution how patient, peaceable, and "safe" the mobs of Petrograd were. The violence came later, with Bolshevism, after the many attempts at counterrevolution, and with vodka. The Bolshevik leaders regret and are ashamed of their red terror. They do not excuse it. It was others, you remember, who traced the worst of the Russian atrocities and the terror itself to the adoption by the counter-revolutionists of the method of assassination (of Lenin and others), and most of all to the discovery by the mobs of wine cellars and vodka stills. That the Russian drunk and the Russian sober are two utterly different animals, is well known to the Jews, to the Reactionaries, and to the Russians themselves. And that is why this people lately have not only obeyed; they have themselves ruthlessly enforced the revolutionary prohibition decrees in every part of Russia that we would inquire about and hear from.

The destructive spirit, sated, exhausted, or suppressed, has done its work. The leaders say so—the leaders of all parties.

There is a close relationship between the Russian people and the new Russian leaders, in power and out. New men in politics are commonly fresh, progressive, representative; it's the later statesmen that damp the enthusiasm and sober the idealism of legislators. In Russia all legislators, all, are young or new. It is as if we should elect in the United States a brand-new set of men to all offices, from the lowest county to the highest Federal position, and as if the election should occur in a great crisis, when all men are full of hope and faith. The new leaders of the local Soviets of Russia were, and they still are, of the people, really. That is one reason why their autocratic dictatorship is acceptable. They have felt, they shared the passion of the mob to destroy, but they had something in mind to destroy.

The soviet leaders used the revolution to destroy the system of organized Russian life.

While the mobs broke windows, smashed wine cellars, and pillaged buildings to express their rage, their leaders directed their efforts to the annihilation of the system itself. They pulled down the Tsar and his officers; they abolished the courts, which had been used to oppress them; they closed shops, stopped business generally, and especially all competitive and speculative business; and they took over all the great industries, monopolies, concessions, and natural resources. This was their purpose. This is their religion. This is what the lower-class culture has been slowly teaching the people of the world for 50 years: that it is not some particular evil, but the whole system of running business and railroads, shops, banks, and exchanges, for speculation and profit that must be changed. This is what causes poverty and riches, they teach, misery, corruption, vice, and war. The people, the workers, or their State, must own and run these things "for service."

Not political democracy, as with us; economic democracy is the idea; democracy in the shop, factory, business. Bolshevism is a literal interpretation, the actual application of this theory, policy, or program. And so, in the destructive period of the Russian revolution, the Bolshevik leaders led the people to destroy the old system, root and branch, fruit and blossom, too. And apparently this was done. The blocks we saw in Petrograd and Moscow of retail shops nailed up were but one sign of it. When we looked back of these dismal fronts and inquired more deeply into the work of the revolution we were convinced that the Russians have literally and completely done their job. And it was this that shocked us. It is this that has startled the world; not the atrocities of the revolution, but the revolution itself.

The organization of life as we know it in America, in the rest of Europe, in the rest of the world, is wrecked and abolished in Russia.

The revolution didn't do it. The Tsar's Government had rotted it. The war broke down the worn-out machinery of it; the revolution has merely scrapped it finally.

The effect is hunger, cold, misery, anguish, disease—death to millions. But worse than these—I mean this—was the confusion of mind among the well and the strong. We do not realize, any of us—even those of us who have imagination—how fixed our minds and habits are by the ways of living that we know. So with the Russians. They understood how to work and live under their old system; it was not a pretty one; it was dark, crooked, and dangerous, but they had groped around in it all their lives from childhood up. They could find their way in it. And now they can remember how it was, and they sigh for the old ways. The rich emigres knew whom to see to bribe for a verdict, a safe-conduct, or a concession; and the poor, in their hunger, think now how it would be to go down to the market and haggle, and bargain, from one booth to another, making their daily purchases, reckoning up their defeats and victories over the traders. And they did get food then.

And now—it is all gone. They have destroyed all this, and having destroyed it they were lost, strangers in their own land.

This tragedy of transition was anticipated by the leaders of the revolution, and the present needs were prepared for in the plans laid for reconstruction.

Lenin has imagination. He is an idealist, but he is a scholar, too, and a very grim realist. Lenin was a statistician by profession. He had long been trying to foresee the future of society under socialism, and he had marked down definitely the resources, the machinery, and the institutions existing under the old order, which could be used in the new. There was the old Russian communal land system, passing, but standing in spots with its peasants accustomed to it. That was to be revived; it is his solution of the problem of the great estates. They are not to be broken up, but worked by the peasants in common. Then there was the great Russian Cooperative (trading) Society, with its 11,000,000 families before the war; now with 17,000,000 members. He kept that. There was a conflict; it was in bourgeoise hands but it was an essential part of the projected system of distribution, so Lenin compromised and communist Russia has it. He had the railroads, telegraph, telephone already; the workers seized the factories, the local Soviets the mines; the All-Russian Soviet, the banks. The new government set up shops—one in each neighborhood—to dole out not for money, but on work tickets, whatever food, fuel, and clothing this complete government monopoly had to distribute. No bargaining, no display, no advertising, and no speculation. Everything one has earned by labor the right to buy at the cooperative and soviet shops is at a fixed, low price, at the established (too small.) profit—to the government or to the members of the cooperative.

Money is to be abolished gradually. It does not count much now. Private capital has been confiscated, most of the rich have left Russia, but there are still many people there who have hidden away money or valuables, and live on them without working. They can buy food and even luxuries, but only illegally from peasants and speculators at the risk of punishment and very high prices. They can buy, also, at the government stores, at the low prices, but they can get only their share there, and only on their class or work tickets. The class arrangement, though transitory and temporary—the aim is to have but one class—is the key to the idea of the whole new system.

There are three classes. The first can buy, for example, 1-1/2 pounds of bread a day; the second, three-quarters of a pound; the third, only one-quarter of a pound; no matter how much money they may have. The first class includes soldiers, workers in war, and other essential industries, actors, teachers, writers, experts, and Government workers of all sorts. The second class is of all other sorts of workers. The third is of people who do not work—the leisure class. Their allowance is, under present circumstances, not enough to live on, but they are allowed to buy surreptitiously from speculators on the theory that the principal of their capital will soon be exhausted, and, since interest, rent, and profits—all forms of unearned money—are abolished, they will soon be forced to go to work.

The shock of this, and the confusion due to the strange details of it, were, and they still are, painful to many minds, and not only to the rich. For a long time there was widespread discontent with this new system. The peasants rebelled, and the workers were suspicious. They blamed the new system for the food shortage, the fuel shortage, the lack of raw materials for the factories. But this also was anticipated by that very remarkable mind and will—Lenin. He used the State monopoly and control of the press, and the old army of revolutionary propagandists to shift the blame for the sufferings of Russia from the revolutionary government to the war, the blockade, and the lack of transportation. Also, he and his executive organization were careful to see that, when the government did get hold of a supply of anything, its arrival was heralded, and the next day it appeared at the community shops, where everybody (that worked) got his share at the low government price. The two American prisoners we saw had noticed this, you remember. "We don't get much to eat," they said, "but neither do our guards or the other Russians. We all get the same. And when they get more, we get our share."

The fairness of the new system, as it works so far, has won over to it the working class and the poorer peasants. The well-to-do still complain, and very bitterly sometimes. Their hoardings are broken into by the government and by the poverty committees, and they are severely punished for speculative trading. But even these classes are moved somewhat by the treatment of children. They are in a class by themselves: class A,—I. They get all the few delicacies—milk, eggs, fruit, game, that

45

come to the government monopoly—at school, where they all are fed, regardless of class. "Even the rich children," they told us, "they have as much as the poor children." And the children, like the workers, now see the operas, too, the plays, the ballets, the art galleries—all with instructors.

The Bolsheviks—all the Russian parties—regard the communists' attitude toward children as the symbol of their new civilization.

"It is to be for the good of humanity, not business," one of them, an American, said, "and the kids represent the future. Our generation is to have only the labor, the joy, and the misery of the struggle. We will get none of the material benefits of the new system, and we will probably never all understand and like it. But the children—it is for them and their children that we are fighting, so we are giving them the best of it from the start, and teaching them to take it all naturally. They are getting the idea. They are to be our new propagandists."

The idea is that everybody is to work for the common good, and so, as the children and the American prisoners note, when they all produce more, they all get more. They are starving now, but they are sharing their poverty. And they really are sharing it. Lenin eats, like everybody else—only one meal a day—soup, fish, bread, and tea. He has to save out of that a bit for breakfast and another bit for supper. The people, the peasants, send him more, but he puts it in the common mess. So the heads of this government do not have to imagine the privations of the people; they feel them. And so the people and the government realize that, if ever Russia becomes prosperous, all will share in the wealth, exactly as they share in the poverty now. In a word, rich Russia expects to become a rich Russian people.

This, then, is the idea which has begun to catch the imagination of the Russian people. This it is that is making men and women work with a new interest, and a new incentive, not to earn high wages and short hours, but to produce an abundance for all. This is what is making a people, sick of war, send their ablest and strongest men into the new, high-spirited, hard-drilled army to defend, not their borders, but their new working system of common living.

And this is what is making Lenin and his sobered communist government ask for peace. They think they have carried a revolution through for once to the logical conclusion. All other revolutions have stopped when they had revolved through the political phase to political democracy. This one has turned once more clear through the economic phase to economic democracy, to self-government in the factory, shop, and on the land, and has laid a foundation for universal profit sharing, for the universal division of food, clothes, and all goods, equally among all. And they think their civilization is working on this foundation. They want time to go on and build it higher and better. They want to spread it all over the world, but only as it works, As they told us when we reminded them that the world dreaded their propaganda:

"We are through with the old propaganda of argument. All we ask now is to be allowed to prove by the examples of things well done here in Russia, that the new system is good. We are so sure we shall make good, that we are willing to stop saying so, to stop reasoning, stop the haranguing, and all that old stuff. And especially are we sick of the propaganda by the sword. We want to stop fighting. We know that each country must evolve its own revolution out of its own conditions and in its own imagination. To force it by war is not scientific, not democratic, not socialistic. And we are fighting now only in self-defense. We will stop fighting, if you will let us stop. We will call back our troops, if you will withdraw yours. We will demobilize. We need the picked organizers and the skilled workers now in the army for our shops, factories, and farms. We would love to recall them to all this needed work, and use their troop trains to distribute our goods and our harvests, if only you will call off your soldiers and your moral, financial, and material support from our enemies, and the enemies of our ideals. Let every country in dispute on our borders self-determine its own form of government and its own allegiance.

"But you must not treat us as a conquered nation. We are not conquered. We are prepared to join in a revolutionary, civil war all over all of Europe and the world, if this good thing has to be done in this bad way of force. But we would prefer to have our time and our energy to work to make sure that our young, good thing is good. We have proved that we can share misery, and sickness, and poverty; it has helped us to have these things to share, and we think we shall be able to share the wealth of Russia as we gradually develop it. But we are not sure of that; the world is not sure. Let us Russians pay the price of the experiment; do the hard, hard work of it; make the sacrifice—then your people can follow us, slowly, as they decide for themselves that what we have is worth having."

That is the message you bring back, Mr. Bullitt. It is your duty to deliver it. It is mine to enforce it by my conception of the situation as it stands in Russia and Europe to-day.

It seems to me that we are on the verge of war, a new war, a terrible war—the long-predicted class war—all over Europe.

The peace commission, busy with the settlement of the old war, may not see the new one, or may not measure aright the imminent danger of it. Germany is going over, Hungary has gone, Austria is coming into the economic revolutionary stage. The propaganda for it is old and strong in all countries: Italy, France, Spain, Belgium, Norway, Sweden—you know. All men know this propaganda. But that is in the rear. Look at the front.

Russia is the center of it. Germany, Austria, Hungary are the wings of the potential war front of—Bolshevism.

And Russia, the center, has made a proposition to you for peace, for a separate peace; made it officially; made it after thought; made it proudly, not in fear, but in pitiful sympathy with its suffering people and for the sake of a vision of the future in which it verily believes. They are practical men—those that made it. You met them. We talked with them. We measured their power. They are all idealists, but they are idealists sobered by the responsibility of power. Sentiment has passed out of them into work—hard work. They said they could give one year more of starvation to the revolution, but they said it practically, and they prefer to compromise and make peace. I believe that, if we take their offer, there will be such an outcry of rage and disappointment from the Left Socialists of Germany, Italy, France, and the world, that Lenin and Trotsky will be astonished. The Red Revolution—the class war—will be broken, and evolution will have its chance once more in the rest of Europe. And you and I know that the men we met in Moscow see this thus, and that they believe the peace conference will not, can not, see it, but will go on to make war and so bring on the European revolution.

But your duty, our duty, is to point out this opportunity, and to vouch for the strength and the will and the character of Lenin and the commissaires of Russia to make and keep the compact they have outlined to you. Well, this is the briefest way in which I can express my full faith:

Kautsky has gone to Moscow. He has gone late; he has gone after we were there. He will find, as we found, a careful, thoughtful, deliberate group of men in power; in too much power; unremovable and controlling a state of monopoly, which is political, social, economic, financial; which controls or directs all the activities, all the fears, all the hopes, all the aspirations of a great people. Kautsky will speak to revolutionary Russia for revolutionary Germany, and for a revolutionary Europe. There will be an appeal in that; there will be a strong appeal in that to the revolutionary Russian commissaires. But, if I am any judge of character, Lenin and his commissaires will stand by their offer to us until Paris has answered, or until the time set for the answer—April 10—shall have passed. Then, and not until then, will Kautsky receive an answer to his appeal for—whatever it is the Germans are asking.

It is not enough that you have delivered your message and made it a part of the record of the peace conference. I think it is your duty to ask the fixed attention of your chiefs upon it for a moment, and to get from them the courtesy of a clear, direct reply to Russia before April 10.

REPORTS OF CAPT. W.W. PETTIT

(The reports of Capt. Pettit are here printed in full, as follows:)

REPORTS OF CAPT, W.W. PETTIT

I left Petrograd on March 31. During the past three weeks I have crossed the Finnish border six times and have been approximately two weeks in Petrograd. I have met Tchitcherin, Litvinov, and most of the important personages in the communist government of Petrograd (including Bill Shatov, chief of police).

Briefly, my opinion of the Russian situation is as follows: In Petrograd I presume the present communist government has a majority of the working-men behind it, but probably less than half of the total population are members of the communist party. However, my conclusions are based on conversations with not only communists, but also many opponents of the communist government, members of the aristocracy, business men, and foreigners, and I am persuaded that a large majority of the population of Petrograd if given a choice between the present government and the two alternatives, revolution or foreign intervention, would without hesitation take the present government. Foreign intervention would unite the population in opposition and would tend to greatly emphasize the present nationalist spirit. Revolution would result in chaos. (There is nowhere a group of Russians in whom the people I have talked with have confidence. Kolchak, Denikin, Yudenvitch, Trepov, the despicable hordes of Russian emigrees who haunt the Grand Hotel, Stockholm; the Socithans House, Helsingfors; the offices of the peace commission in Paris, and squabble among themselves as to how the Russian situation shall be solved; all equally fail to find many supporters in Petrograd.) Those with whom I have talked recognize that revolution, did it succeed in developing a strong government, would result in a white terror comparable with that of Finland. In Finland our consul has a record of 12,500 executions in some 50 districts, out of something like 500 districts, by the White Guard. In Petrograd I have been repeatedly assured that the total Red executions in Petrograd and Moscow and other cities was at a maximum 3,200.

It may seem somewhat inconsistent for the Russian bourgeoisie to oppose allied intervention and at the same time fail to give whole-hearted support to the present government. They justify this attitude on the grounds that when the two great problems of food and peace are solved the whole population can turn itself to assisting the present régime in developing a stable efficient government. They point to the numerous changes which have already been introduced by the present communist government, to the acknowledgment that mistakes have been made to the ease of securing introduction of constructive ideas under the present régime. All these facts have persuaded many of the thinking people with whom I have talked to look to the present government in possibly a somewhat modified form as the salvation of Russia.

At present the situation is bad. Russia is straining every nerve to raise an army to oppose the encircling White Guards. That the army is efficient is demonstrated by the present location of Soviet forces who have contended with the Russian White Guard supported by enormous sums of money, munitions, and even soldiers from the Allies. Naturally, transportation is inefficient; it was horrible in the last year of the Czar's regime. Absolute separation from the rest of the world, combined with the chaotic conditions which Russia has passed through since the 1917 revolution, plus the sabotage, which until recently was quite general among the intelligent classes, including engineers, has resulted in a decrease in rolling stock. The transportation of the enormous army which has been raised limits the number of cars which can be used for food. The cutting off of Siberia, Finland, the Baltic Provinces, and until recently the Ukraine, made it necessary to establish new lines of food transportation. Consequently there has been great suffering in Petrograd. Of the population of a million, 200,000 are reported by the board of health to be ill, 100,000 seriously ill in hospitals or at home, and another 100,000 with swollen limbs still able to go to the food kitchens. However, the reports of people dying in the streets are not true. Whatever food exists is fairly well distributed and there are food kitchens where anyone can get a fairly good dinner for 3.50 rubles.

For money one can still obtain many of the luxuries of life. The children, some 50,000 of whom have been provided with homes, are splendidly taken care of, and except for the absence of milk have little to complain of. In the public schools free lunches are given the children, and one sees in the faces of the younger generation little of the suffering which some of the older people have undergone and are undergoing. Food conditions have improved recently, due to the suspension of passenger traffic and the retaking of the Ukraine, where food is plentiful. From 60 to 100 carloads of food have arrived in Petrograd each day since February 18.

Perhaps it is futile to add that my solution of the Russian problem is some sort of recognition of the present government, with the establishment of economic relations and the sending of every possible assistance to the people. I have been treated in a wonderful manner by the communist representatives, though they know that I am no socialist and though I have admitted to the leaders that my civilian clothing is a disguise. They have the warmest affection for America, believe in President Wilson, and are certain that we are coming to their assistance, and, together with our engineers, our food, our school-teachers, and our supplies, they are going to develop in Russia a government which will emphasize the rights of the common people as no other government has. I am so convinced of the necessity for us taking a step immediately to end the suffering of this wonderful people that I should be willing to stake all I have in converting ninety out of every hundred American business men whom I could take to Petrograd for two weeks.

It is needless for me to tell you that most of the stories that have come from Russia regarding atrocities, horrors, immorality, are manufactured in Viborg, Helsingfors, or Stockholm. The horrible massacres planned for last November were first learned of in Petrograd from the Helsingfors papers. That anybody could even for a moment believe in the nationalization of women seems impossible to anyone in Petrograd. To-day Petrograd is an orderly city—probably the only city of the world of its size without police. Bill Shatov, chief of police, and I were at the opera the other night to hear Chaliapine sing in Boris Gudonov. He excused himself early because he said there had been a robbery the previous night, in which a man had lost 5,000 rubles, that this was the first robbery in several weeks, and that he had an idea who had done it, and was going to get the men that night. I feel personally that Petrograd is safer than Paris. At night there are automobiles, sleighs, and people on the streets at 12 o'clock to a much greater extent than was true in Paris when I left five weeks ago.

Most wonderful of all, the great crowd of prostitutes has disappeared. I have seen not a disreputable woman since I went to Petrograd, and foreigners who have been there for the last three months report the same. The policy of the present government has resulted in eliminating throughout Russia, I am told, this horrible outgrowth of modern civilization.

Begging has decreased. I have asked to be taken to the poorest parts of the city to see how the people in the slums live, and both the communists and bourgeoisie have held up their hands and said, "But you fail to understand there are no such places." There is poverty, but it is scattered and exists among those of the former poor or of the former rich who have been unable to adapt themselves to the conditions which require everyone to do something.

Terrorism has ended. For months there have been no executions, I am told, and certainly people go to the theater and church and out on the streets as much as they would in any city of the world.

(Certain memoranda referred to in the hearing relating to the work of Capt. Pettit in Russia are here printed in full as follows:)

MEMORANDUM

From: W.W. Pettit

To: Ammission, Paris.

(Attention of Mr. Bullitt.)

1. *Mr. Pettit's recent movements.*—On March 18 I left Helsingfors for Petrograd and remained there until March 28 when I left for Helsingfors, at which place I received a cable ordering me to report immediately to Paris. On the 29th I left again for Petrograd to secure some baggage I had left. On the 21st I left Petrograd for Helsingfors. On April 1st I left Helsingfors for Stockholm and in Stockholm I find a telegram asking me to wait until I receive further orders.

2. *Optimism of present government.*—On the night of the 30th and the afternoon of the 31st I had several hours with Schklovsky, Tchitcherin's personal representative in Petrograd. He was disappointed to think I was to return to Paris, but felt certain that inasmuch as the orders recalling me had been sent before Mr. Bullitt's arrival, there was every possibility of my being returned to Petrograd. He was most optimistic about the future and felt that the Allies must soon take some definite stand regarding Russia, and that the result of the Paris negotiations would almost surely be favorable to the Soviet Government. He said that the present war conditions and the limited transportation facilities, with the shortage of food resulting therefrom, had handicapped his government enormously, and that everyone hopes that soon the action of the allied powers will permit the establishment of normal relations in Russia.

3. *Radios in re Bullitt.*—He has received at least three radio communications from the American press in which Mr. Bullitt's activities have been mentioned and this has tended to encourage him. The last cablegram stated that Mr. Bullitt was preparing a statement regarding conditions in Russia which the press anticipated would go far toward dispelling ignorance and misinformation regarding conditions in Moscow and Petrograd.

4. *Hungarian situation.*—The Hungarian situation has also gone far toward encouraging the present Government. Hungary has proposed a mutual offensive and defensive alliance with Russia. The fact that the Soviet Government has been instituted in Hungary without bloodshed up to the present, and with little opposition on the part of the people, has also encouraged Schklovsky. He stated that the action of the Allies in sending troops against Hungary was to be regretted because of

49

the bloodshed which would probably result. However, he thought in the long run that the Allies would find it a suicidal policy to try to suppress the Hungarian revolution by force.

5. *The Ukraine situation.*—The soviet troops have taken almost the entire Ukraine and this with the food supplies which it will provide have strengthened the Soviet Government. A friend who has recently returned from Peltava, Ekaterinoslav, Kiev, and other southern cities, states that food is abundant and cheap. The Soviet Government believes that the French and Greek troops are withdrawing from Odessa and going to Sebastopol. They anticipate taking Odessa within the next few days.

6. *Esthonian situation.*—At least twice within the last two weeks Esthonia has sent word to the Soviet Government that it desired peace. The following four points have been emphasized by the Esthonians: (1) That peace must come immediately; (2) that the offer must come from the Soviet Government; (3) that a fair offer will be accepted by the Esthonians immediately without consultation with France or England, who are supporting them; (4) that free access to Esthonian harbors and free use of Esthonian railroads will be assured the Soviet Government.

7. *The Lithuanian situation.*—It is fairly well understood that the Lithuanian Government that is fighting the Bolsheviks is not going to allow itself to be made a tool by the French and British Governments to invade Russian territory. The Lithuanian Government is desirous of securing possession of Lithuanian territory, but beyond that it is understood it will not go.

8. *The Finnish situation.*—The Soviet Government is in close touch with the Finnish situation and has little fear of an invasion of Russia from that direction. The Finnish Army is without question a third Red; probably a half Red; possibly two-thirds Red. There is even reported to be a tendency on a part of certain of the White Guards to oppose intervention in Russia. One of the Finnish regiments in Esthonia has returned to Finland, and it is supposed that it will assist the proposed revolution of the Finns in East Karelia against the Soviet Government. The Soviet Government has sent a committee to Helsingfors to arrange economic relations with Finland, and it is said that this committee carries threats of reprisals on the part of the Soviet Government against the Finns in Petrograd unless the treaty is negotiated. It is said in Petrograd that some of the Finns have already left Petrograd in anticipation that the Finnish Government will not be permitted to make any arrangement with the Soviet Government because of the attitude of certain of the allied representatives in Helsingfors.

9. *Improvement in food conditions.*—The suspension of passenger traffic from March 18 to April 10 has resulted in the Government bringing to Petrograd 60 to 100 cars of food each day, and one sees large quantities of food being transported about the city. At Easter time it is hoped to be able to give 3 pounds of white bread to the population of Petrograd. There also seems to be a larger supply of food for private purchase in the city. Mr. Shiskin has recently been able to buy 3 geese, a sucking pig, 2 splendid legs of veal, and roasts of beef at from 40 to 50 rubles a pound, which, considering the value of the ruble, is much less than it sounds. Shiskin has also been able recently to get eggs, milk, honey, and butter, together with potatoes, carrots, and cabbage. My bill for food for 11 days with Mr. Shiskin was about 1,300 rubles.

10. *Order in Petrograd.*—About three weeks ago there were several strikes in factories in Petrograd and Lenin came to talk to the strikers. Apparently the matter was settled satisfactorily and the workers were given the same bread rations that the soldiers receive. At the Putilov works some 400 men struck and part of them were dismissed. Both Shatov and the director of factories said that there were no executions, though the population the next morning reported 80 workers shot and that afternoon the rumor had increased the number to 400. There is practically no robbery in the city. Shatov left the opera the other night early because he told me the previous night a man had lost 5,000 rubles and it was such an exceptional thing to have a robbery that he was going out personally to investigate the matter, having some idea as to who was responsible.

11. *Currency plans.*—Zorin tells me that the Soviet Government has or had printed a new issue of currency which it is proposed to exchange for the old currency within the next three months. The details of the plan have not been completed but he thinks that an exchange of ruble for ruble will be made up to 3,000; an additional 2,000 will be placed on deposit in the government bank. That beyond 5,000 only a small percentage will be allowed to any one, and that a limit of possibly 15,000 will be placed beyond which no rubles will be exchanged. Then the plan is, after a certain period to declare the old ruble valueless. Zorin feels that as a result of this plan the new ruble will

have some value and that the present situation in the country in which the farmer has so much paper that he refuses to sell any longer for money, will be relieved. This exchange would be followed later on by the issue of still other currency the entire purpose being the more equal distribution of wealth and the gradual approach to elimination of currency.

12. *Concessions.*—It is asserted that the northern railway concession has been signed and Amundsen tells me that all negotiations were accomplished without the payment of a single cent of tea money, probably the first instance of the absence of graft in such negotiations in the history of Russia. He says that Trepov, through his agent Borisov, at Moscow, was the greatest opponent of the Norwegian interests. Trepov was formerly minister of ways and communications and is reported to have been refused a similar concession under the Czar's government. Amundsen claims that Trepov has made every effort to secure this concession from the Soviet Government. I am attaching a statement regarding a concession which is supposed to have been granted to the lumber interests. There are rumors that other concessions have been granted.

13. *Y.M.C.A.*—Recently the Y.M.C.A. secretary arrived in Petrograd, claiming to have come without authorization from his superiors. He has been staying at the embassy but recently went to Moscow at the invitation of Tchitcherin. Schklovsky tells me that the American has plans for the establishment of the Y.M.C.A. in Russia which he wanted to put before the Moscow government. Schklovsky doubted that it would be feasible to organize in Russia at present a branch of the International association unless some rather fundamental modifications were made in their policy.

14. *Treadwell.*—I have twice asked Schklovsky to secure information regarding Treadwell, and he assures me that he has taken the matter up with Moscow, but that apparently they have had no news from Tashkent as yet. He promised to let me know as soon as anything was heard.

15. *Attitude toward United States.*—The degree of confidence which the Russians and the soviet officials show toward our Government is to me a matter of surprise, considering our activities during the past 18 months. There seems to be no question in the minds of the officials in Petrograd whom I have met that we are going to give them an opportunity to develop a more stable form of government, and they apparently look upon President Wilson as one who is going to decide the question on its merits without being influenced by the enormous pressure of the Russian emigrés and the French Government. Doubtless part of this attitude is due to the favorable impression created by Mr. Bullitt, but much of it must be the result of information which they have secured from the press. At the present moment the United States has the opportunity of demonstrating to the Russian people its friendship and cementing the bonds which already exist. Russia believes in us, and a little assistance to Russia in its present crisis will result in putting the United States in a position in Russia which can never be overthrown by Germany or any other power.

16. *Social work.*—I have recently sent a cable from Helsingfors regarding health and sanitary conditions in Petrograd, a copy of which I am attaching. I have spent the past two weeks visiting schools and the children's home in Petrograd. There are 30,000 children for whom homes have been provided in the past nine months, and preparations are being made to house 10,000 more. Homes of emigrés are being taken over and groups of 40 children placed in them under the care of able instructors; where the children are old enough they go to school during the daytime. A beautiful home life has been developed. The children are well fed and well clothed, and there is a minimum of sickness among them. At the present time, when so much disease exists in Petrograd, and when there is so much starvation, the healthy appearance of these thousands of children, together with the well-fed condition of children who are not in institutions, but are receiving free meals in schools, is a demonstration of the social spirit behind much of the activities of the present government. I shall send later a more detailed statement of some of the interesting things I have learned about this phase of the activities of the new regime.

17. *Conclusion.*—In this rather hastily dictated memorandum which Mr. Francis is going to take tonight to Paris I have tried to point out some of the things that have interested me in Petrograd. Naturally I have emphasized the brighter side, for the vast amount of absolutely false news manufactured in Helsingfors and Stockholm and sent out through the world seems to me to necessitate the emphasizing of some of the more hopeful features of the present government. Naturally the character of the Russian people has not changed to any great extent in 18 months, and there is doubtless corruption, and there is certainly inefficiency and ignorance and a hopeless failure to grasp the new principles motivating the government on the part of many of the people. A people

subjected to the treatment which Russians have had during the last 200 years can not in one generation be expected to change very greatly, but personally I feel the present government has made a vast improvement on the government of the Czar as I knew it in 1916-17. Without doubt the majority of the people in Petrograd are opposed to allied intervention or revolution and wish the present government to be given a fair chance to work out the salvation of Russia. One of the most hopeful symptoms of the present government is its willingness to acknowledge mistakes when they are demonstrated and to adopt new ideas which are worth while. Personally I am heart and soul for some action on the part of the United States Government which will show our sincere intention to permit the Russian people to solve their own problems with what assistance they may require from us. STOCKHOLM, April 4 1919.

SOCIAL WORK IN PETROGRAD

The wife of Zinoviev, Madame Lelina, is in charge of the social institutions in the city of Petrograd. This does not include the public schools, which are under another organization. Madame Lelina is a short-haired woman, probably Jewish, of about 45. She has an enormous amount of energy, and is commonly supposed to be doing at least two things at the same time. The morning I met her she was carrying on two interviews and trying to arrange to have me shown some of the social work she is directing. There seemed to be little system about her efforts. Her office was rather disorderly, and her method of work seemed very wasteful of time and effort, and very much like the usual Russian way of doing things. Bill Shatov, formerly organizer of the I.W.W., who is commissar of police for Petrograd and also commissar for one of the northern armies, introduced me to Madame Lelina, and accompanied me the first day on our visits. We were guided by a young woman by the name of Bachrath, who is a university graduate and lawyer, and since the legal profession has fallen into disrepute, has turned her efforts toward social work.

Under her guidance I spent three days visiting institutions. I saw a boarding school for girls, a boarding home for younger children, an institution for the feeble-minded, three of the new homes organized by the Soviet Government, and two small hospitals for children.

The institutions which Madame Lelina is directing are in two groups: First, those which she has taken over from the old Czar regime, and second, those which have been founded in the last 18 months. The new government has been so handicapped by the difficulties of securing food and other supplies, by the sabotage of many of the intelligent classes, and by the necessity of directing every energy toward carrying on hostilities against the bourgeoisie and the Allies, that there has been little opportunity to remodel the institutions inherited from the previous régime, therefore neither the strength nor the weakness of these institutions is to any great extent due to the present régime. Two of the institutions I visited were of this type, one happened to be very good and the other very bad, and in neither case did I feel that Lelina's organization was responsible.

An aristocratic organization under the Czar maintained a boarding school for girls. This has been taken over by the Soviet Government with little change, and the 140 children in this institution are enjoying all the opportunities which a directress trained in France and Germany, with an exceptionally skillful corps of assistants, can give them.

I inquired regarding the changes which the Soviet Government had made in the organization of this school. Some of the girls who were there have been kept, but vacant places have been filled by Madame Lelina's committee, and the institution has been required to take boys into the day school, a plan which is carried out in most of the soviet social and educational work. Much more freedom has been introduced in the management of the institution, and the girls at table talk and walk about, much as though they were in their own homes. The Soviet Government requires that certain girls be permitted membership in the teachers' committee, and the two communists accompanying me pointed to this as a great accomplishment. Privately, the teachers informed me they regarded it as of little significance, and apparently they were entirely out of sympathy with the innovations that the new government has made. Now all the girls are required to work in the kitchen, dining room, or m cleaning their own dormitories, and certain girls are assigned to the kitchen to over-see the use of supplies by the cooks. However, the whole institution, from the uniforms of the girls to the required form in which even hand towels have to be hung, indicates the iron will of the directress. In one class we visited the girls sat at desks and listened to a traditional pedagogue pour out quantities of information on Pushkin's Boris Gudonov. Occasionally the girls were called upon to react, which they did with sentences apparently only partially memorized. The spirit of the institution is behind that of our better institutions in America, and the spirit of the classroom is quite mediaeval.

The greatest objection which the teachers seem to have to soviet activities is the question of sacred pictures and religious observances. The chapel of the school has been closed, but in each room from the corner still hangs the Ikon and at the heads of many of the girls' beds there are still small pictures of the Virgin, much to the disgust of the representatives of the Soviet Government, who in many cases are Jewish, and in practically all cases have renounced any religious connection. Recently the Soviet Party has announced the fact that they as a party are not hostile to any religion, but intend to remain neutral on the subject. The attitude of the commissars apparently is that required religious observances should not be permitted in public institutions, and doubtless some of the inspectors have gone further than was necessary in prohibiting any symbol of the religion which probably most of the children still nominally adhere to.

The second institution I visited, which had been taken over from the old government, was an orphan asylum with some 600 children mostly under 10. It was frightfully crowded, in many places rather dirty, with frequently bad odors from unclean toilets. In one little room some 20 small boys were sleeping and eating, and I found one child of 2 who was not able to walk and was eating in the bed in which he slept.

Ventilation was bad, linen not very clean, a general feeling of repression present, slovenly employees, and, in general, an atmosphere of inefficiency and failure to develop a home spirit which one still finds in some of the worst institutions in America. The instructor who showed me this home realized its horrors, and said that the Government intended to move the children into more adequate quarters as soon as conditions permitted. In summer the children are all taken to the country. In this institution all the older children go out to public schools and there have been no cases of smallpox or typhus in spite of the epidemics the city has had this winter. Forty children were in the hospital with minor complaints. About 10 per cent of the children are usually ill.

The school for feeble-minded occupies a large apartment house and the children are divided into groups of 10 under the direction of two teachers, each group developing home life in one of the large apartments. There is emphasis on handwork. Printing presses, a bookbinding establishment, and woodworking tools are provided. Music and art appreciation are given much time, and some of the work done is very beautiful. This school is largely the result of the efforts of the Soviet Government. Careful records are kept of the children and simple test material has been devised to develop in the more backward children elementary reactions regarding size, shape, form, and color. The greatest difficulty is the impossibility of securing trained workers either for the shops or for the special pedagogical problems of the school. However, an energetic corps of young men and young women are employed, and they are conscious of the size of their problem and are already thinking of the difficulties of sending their students back into industrial life. In many of the activities of the Soviet Government, as well as in these institutions taken over from the old regime, I was dismayed at the inefficiency and ignorance of many of the subordinates. After talking to the leaders and getting some understanding of their ideals, an American expects to see these carried over into practice. One is liable to forget that the Russian people have not greatly changed, and that the same easy-going, inefficient attitude of decades of the previous regime still exists. No one knows this obstacle better than the members of the present regime. They realize that the character of the Russian people is their greatest obstacle, and change in the Russian conception of Government service is a slow process. Far from being discouraged, they point to their accomplishments with pride.

During the last nine months Madame Lelina has taken 30,000 children into Government homes and preparations are made to take 10,000 more during the next three months. The three new institutions which I visited are attractive suburban homes of wealthy emigrés. The Government has taken these over and is putting groups of 40 children in charge of specially selected and trained men and women. The older children go out to school. For the younger children kindergarten activities are provided and much time is spent out of doors. An atmosphere of home life has been developed which is surprising considering the short time the institutions have been organized and the difficulties they have had to contend with. This plan, which I am told is permanent, is a most encouraging feature of Madame Lelina's work.

53

Requests to have children placed in the Government institutions are turned over to a special corps of investigators. In each house there is what is known as a poor committee which must also approve the requests and the local soviet is required to pass upon the commitment of the child to an institution. The large number of children taken over by the city is due to the number of orphans and half orphans caused by the war and to the impossibility of many poor families providing their children with food during the recent famine. In cases where several children of a family are taken they are placed in the same home. Frequent opportunities for relatives to visit the homes are provided. The amount of sickness has been surprisingly low considering the great amount of disease in Petrograd during the last few months. In one group of 300 children there have been no deaths within the past nine months, and among all the children there have been very few cases of contagious diseases.

The difficulties which Madame Lelina faces are numerous. First, Russia has never had an adequate number of trained workers and many of those who were trained have refused to cooperate with the present regime, and, secondly, though the Soviet Government has adopted the policy of turning over to the children's homes and the schools an adequate supply of food, regardless of the suffering of the adult population, still it has been impossible to get certain items of diet, as, for instance, milk. It is true, however, that among these children one sees few signs of undernourishment or famine, and in general throughout the city the children seem much better nourished than the adult population.

I had planned to visit other institutions but was unable to do so. I was told of a large palace which has been taken over as a home for mothers. Here all women who so desire are sent after childbirth with their children for a period of two months.

The health department, which asserts that there are in addition to the 100,000 bedridden people in the city, another 100,000 who are ill because of undernourishment though able to go to the food kitchens, has been very successful in securing from the local soviets special food supplies to be provided sick persons on doctors' orders. At each food kitchen the board of health has a representative whose business it is to give such special diet as may be possible to undernourished individuals.

(Thereupon, at 12.50 o'clock p.m., the committee adjourned subject to the call of the chairman.)

Made in the USA
Las Vegas, NV
19 November 2024